CO-AZJ-232

The Gourmet
and
The Camera

The Gourmet and The Camera

Culinary Treasures from Around the World

By
CORALYNN HILL

Westover
Publishing Company
An Affiliate of Media General, Richmond, Virginia

Prepared in Cooperation with
Photo Researchers, Inc.
New York, New York

First Edition. Library of Congress Catalogue
Card Number 79-161079.

"The history of the table of a nation is a reflection of the civilization of that nation."

AUGUSTE ESCOFFIER

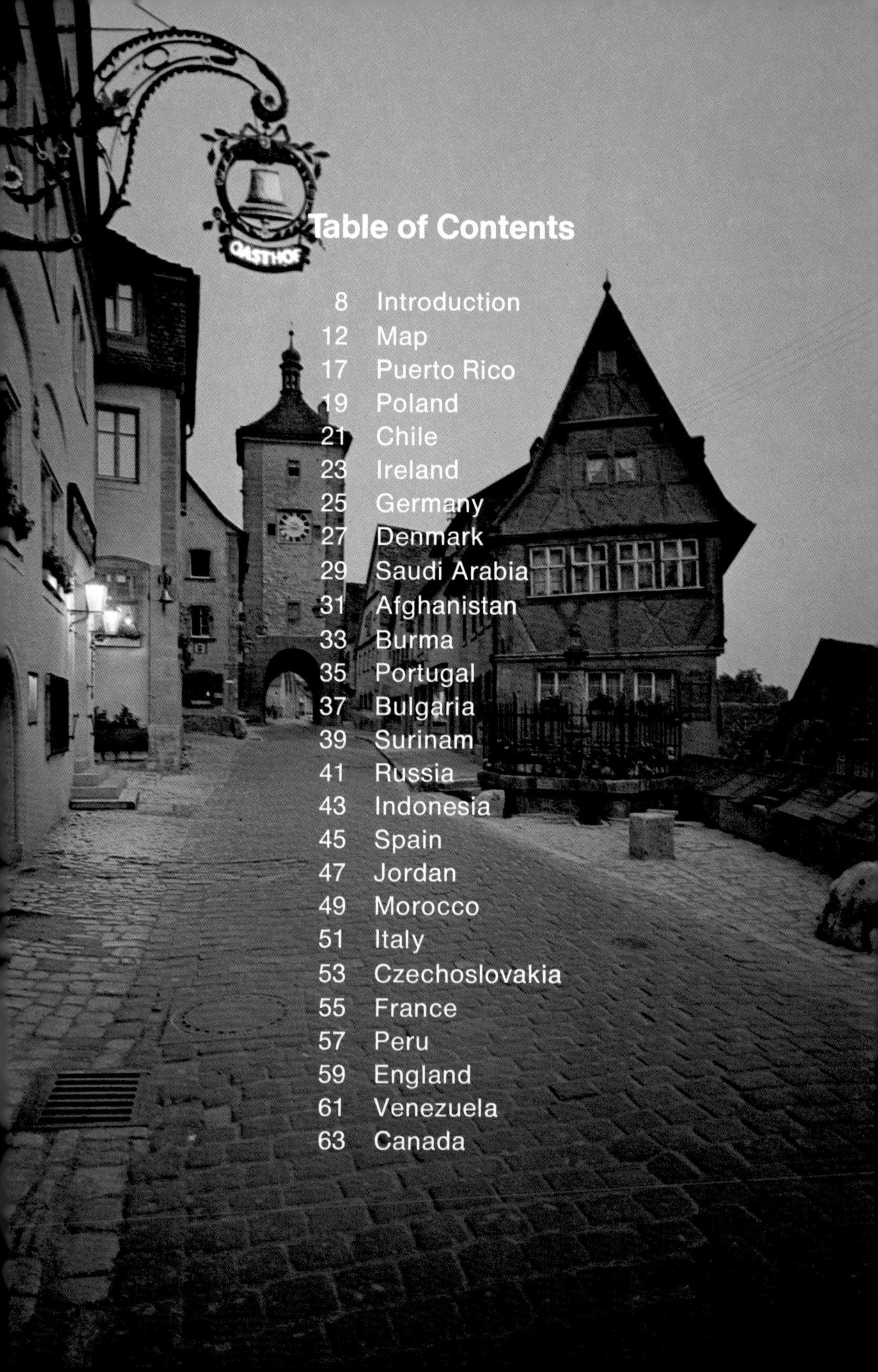

Table of Contents

GASTHOF

INTRODUCTION

ALTHOUGH I could not hope to pass as even a part-time jetsetter, one of my most pleasurable pastimes is traveling, particularly to those countries outside the United States. It's not that I'm unpatriotic, but I grew up outside the United States, and since my parents always seemed to be off on some junket—inevitably with me tagging along—I developed the wanderlust habit very early.

My father was an American working in England, and my mother was French. There were some Italian and German aunts and uncles, and while the language and accents of my relatives sometimes gave me traumas, the food at our family gatherings could always be counted on to provide a common ground of camaraderie. If you have never been to an international family reunion, you have missed an experience that would throw the president of Alka Seltzer into paroxysms of joy. It's one thing to sit down to a feast featuring turkey, dressing, and baked potatoes; it's quite another to sit down to one featuring spaghetti, red cabbage, and kidney pie. Somehow, however, I survived the wide variety and frequent changes of foods during my formulative years, and even began to thrive on international fare.

When I first started traveling on my own, invariably upon returning from a trip abroad, I would remember particularly impressing eating experiences and rush immediately to my cookbook shelves, hoping to recreate them. The mess I usually concocted had little relation to what I remembered, and tastebuds aquiver, I would immediately start planning another trip.

Now, whenever I eat something I like, I ask for the recipe —no matter where I am. Sometimes I'm refused, but more often a chef is only too glad to share the secrets of his personal masterpieces with an admiring foreigner. Often I must have such mouth-watering formulas translated upon returning home, but that's all part of the fun.

All my friends know of this habit, and every time I return from a jaunt, it seems that everyone I know calls. After the usual pleasantries, they hem and haw for a bit, and then pop the inevitable questions: "Where did you eat?" and "What recipes did you bring back?" If my friends are that interested, the general public seems more so. During and since World War II, countless American soldiers have brought home the joys of foreign foods that provided them welcome relief from their rations and tasteless army fare. In more recent years, increased travel and communication have put the entire world within our reach, and nothing seems to excite us more about our foreign neighbors than their food. International cookbooks sell hundreds of thousands of copies, food distributors are daily besieged with requests to market more and more imported food products, and cooking schools which specialize in foreign foods are becoming more and more popular.

In the large metropolitan areas that have provided new homes for thousands of immigrants, foreign food markets and restaurants abound. In New York, for instance, one can partake of almost any food from any land, large or small, well-known or obscure. But outside these areas, we are still fairly much restricted in our culinary pursuits. Of the foreign restaurants we tend to frequent, or that are available to us, most are of only several national origins. So if all of us are to expand our horizons in the area of international cuisine, it is obvious that, to a great extent, we are on our own, and must pursue our course through travel and related endeavors.

Wanting to make some small contribution to the understanding and enjoyment of international cuisine, I spent months trying to determine what I could do that would be appealing—as well as new and intriguing. Then one night I was a guest at a diplomatic dinner held by a foreign embassy. As conversations in at least ten different languages surrounded me, I pondered over what would be served to this distinguished and diverse group. What would the embassy's chef consider his most delectable offering from the representative dishes of his native country? The answer to that question came to me at about the same time as did the idea for this book.

For the next six months, I made it my task to write representatives of many different countries—all the ones you might expect, as well as many that would provide the unusual and exotic. From each, I asked for one or several of their most representative national dishes. Their response was overwhelming, and their excitement for the project almost equal to my own. Many of the recipes were graciously provided by the embassies of the countries, and represent those dishes so prized that they are regularly served at official diplomatic and state dinners. Others have been contributed by national tourist bureaus as particularly indicative of the countries' culinary traditions. Still others come from the chefs and kitchens of some of the most famous hotels and restaurants of every continent. Each recipe proved as enjoyable as the next, and my diligent testing of all only proved that a person could grow happily fat while preparing a cookbook.

That explanation accounts for the "gourmet" part of the book. The "and the Camera" part followed naturally. As I received recipes, each seemed to bring back memories and images of eating those dishes in the best possible circumstances—surrounded by their own native scenery, mood, and traditions. I remembered eating paella cooked over an open fire with a group of Spanish friends . . . wolfing down what seemed at the time to be tons of cheese fondue in a cozy ski lodge high in the Alps . . . sopping up portion after portion of Irish stew amidst the raucous conviviality of a Dublin tavern. Obviously, something more than just recipes was needed to give the book life. Photographs provided the answer, and each has been chosen to offer what I hope is a perfect background for each country and dish.

Readers of THE GOURMET AND THE CAMERA will note that all the dishes featured are main courses. Leaving out accompaniments will, I hope, stimulate your own imagination and ingenuity. In planning your menus around the recipes in the book, there are only two guidelines that are really important: First, simplicity and ease are always the best policies, and second, nothing is wrong that you and your guests enjoy.

Prior to each recipe, a list of necessary ingredients has been given to provide you with at-a-glance marketing information. As in the case of all recipes, however, you should read through each fully before beginning your preparation.

I hope THE GOURMET AND THE CAMERA will evoke vivid reminiscences for the world traveler, and open new vistas for all in the area of international cuisine. I also hope that the book is as much fun to use as it was to research and compile.

Coralynn Hill

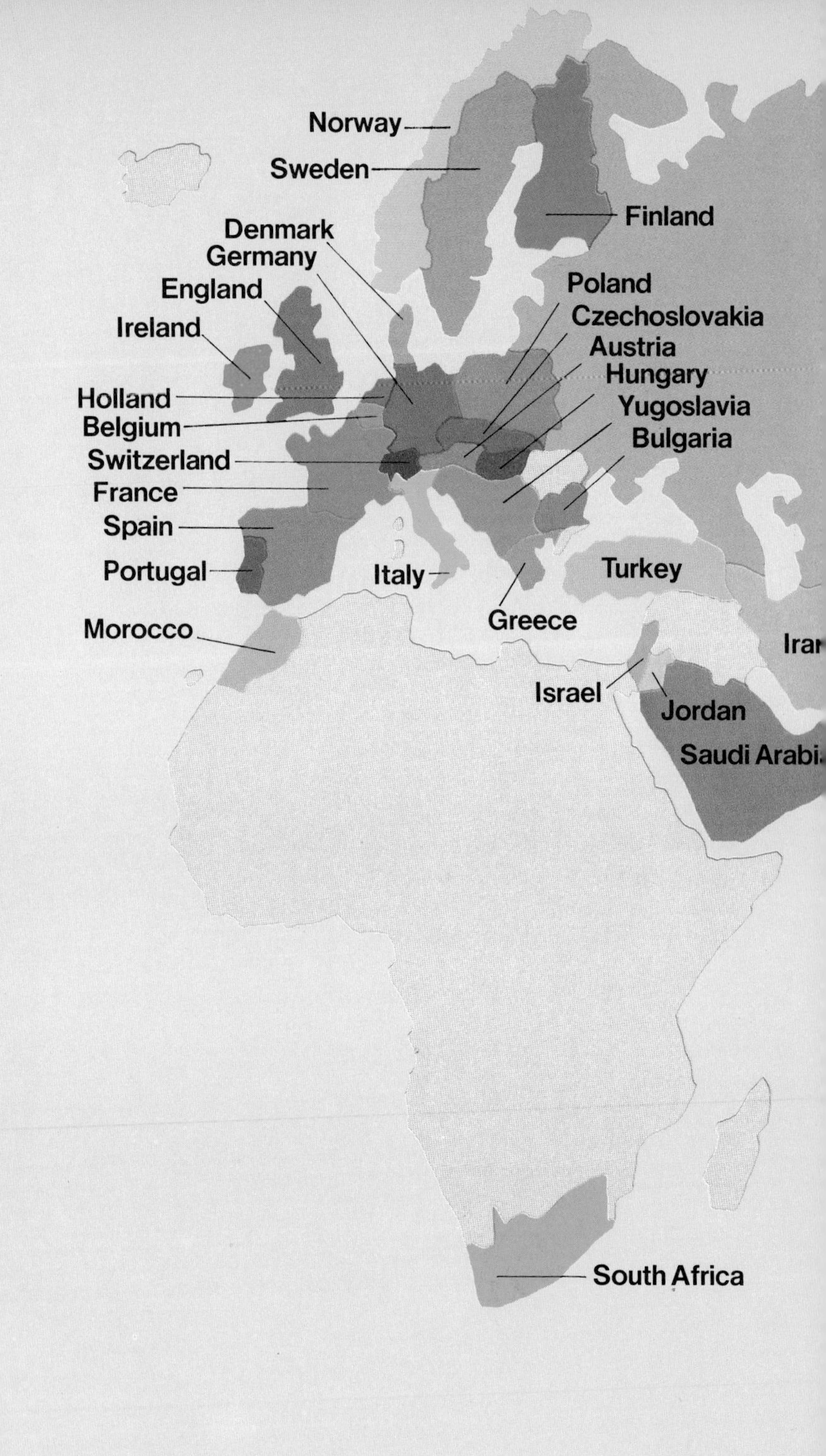

Norway
Sweden
Finland
Denmark
Germany
England
Ireland
Poland
Czechoslovakia
Austria
Hungary
Yugoslavia
Bulgaria
Holland
Belgium
Switzerland
France
Spain
Portugal
Italy
Turkey
Morocco
Greece
Israel
Jordan
Saudi Arabi
Irar
South Africa

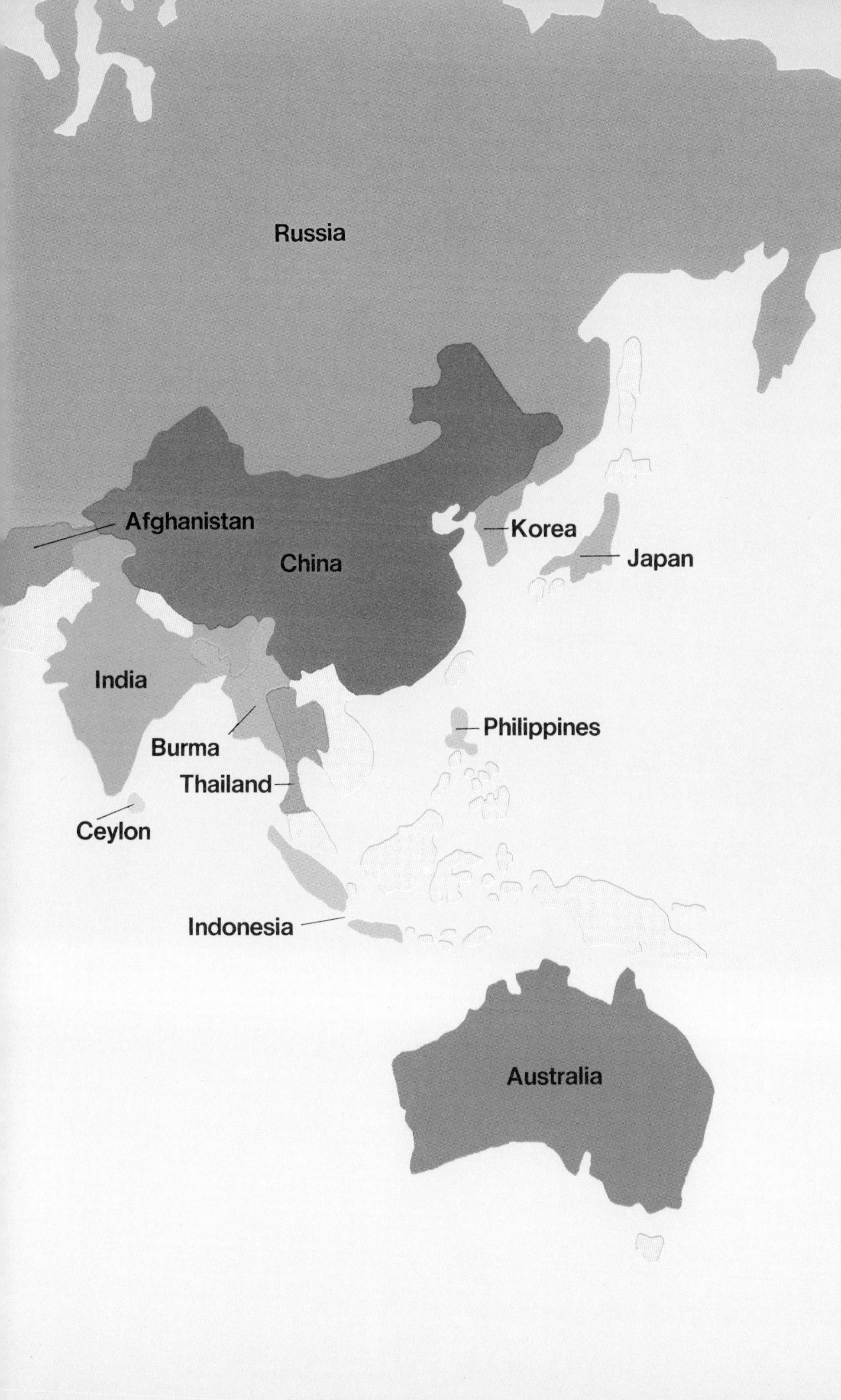
Russia
Afghanistan
China
Korea
Japan
India
Burma
Thailand
Ceylon
Philippines
Indonesia
Australia

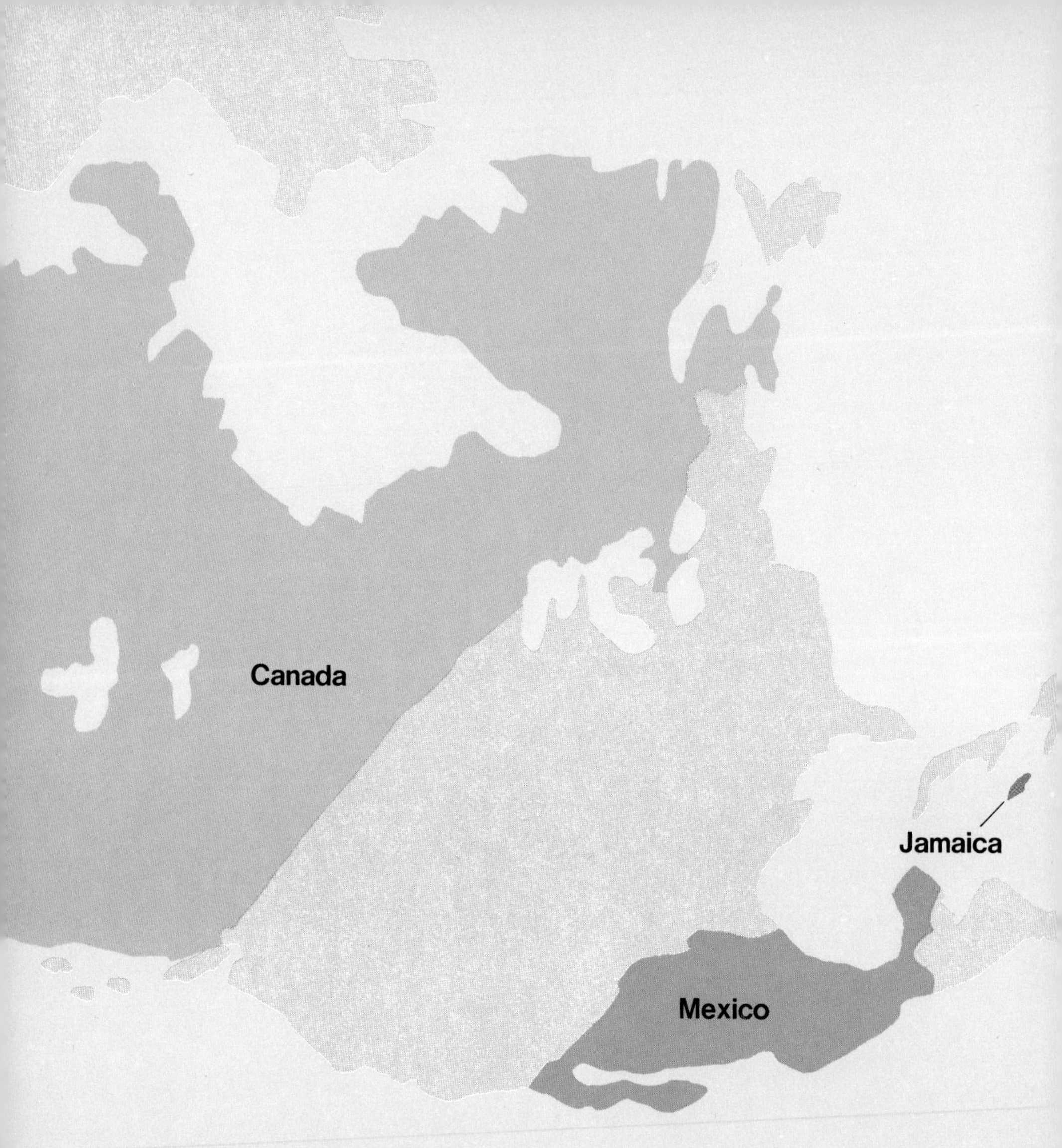

Canada

Jamaica

Mexico

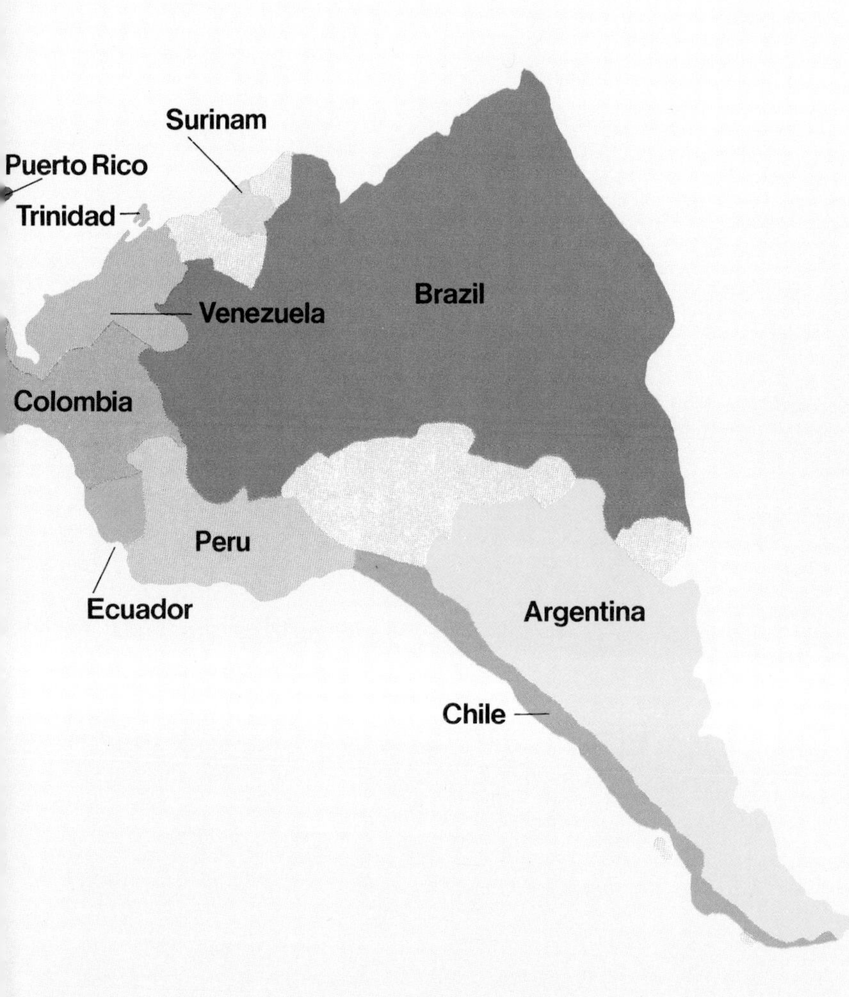
Surinam
Puerto Rico
Trinidad
Brazil
Venezuela
Colombia
Peru
Ecuador
Argentina
Chile

Caribbean Beach, Puerto Rico

PUERTO RICO

LANGOSTA A LA CRIOLLA-ESTILO PUERTORRIQUENO (Lobster Creole)

YOU WILL NEED: onions, green peppers, garlic, olive oil, salt, pepper, tomatoes, tomato sauce, lobster, white cooking wine.

2 medium onions, chopped
2 large green peppers, chopped
2 cloves garlic, minced
½ cup olive oil
1½ teaspoon salt
½ teaspoon pepper
2 medium fresh tomatoes, peeled, cored, and quartered
2 8-ounce cans tomato sauce
2 pounds cooked lobster meat, cut into small pieces
½ cup white cooking wine

Sauté the onions, green peppers, and garlic in the olive oil until tender. Add the salt, pepper and the fresh tomatoes, and cook until the tomatoes are soft. Stir in the tomato sauce and the lobster meat, and simmer for 15 minutes. Add the white wine, and cook for 2 to 3 minutes longer. Serve over cooked rice.

Serves 6.

Zakopane, Poland

POLAND

ZRAZY A LA NELSON II

YOU WILL NEED: butter, onion, bouillon, mushrooms, potatoes, veal, salt, pepper, sour cream, red wine.

Butter
1 onion, chopped
2 pounds veal
1 glass red wine
4 fresh mushrooms, chopped
1 cup bouillon broth
1 package dried mushrooms, soaked and chopped
2 pounds potatoes
2 tablespoons sour cream
Salt and pepper to taste

Melt 1 tablespoon of butter and brown in it a finely chopped onion. When the onion gets rosy-colored, add the bouillon broth and chopped mushrooms. Pour glass of red wine and 1 cup of the mushroom broth from dried mushrooms after mushrooms have been removed. Simmer. Cook the potatoes separately. Slice the meat into thin cutlets; pound it. Season the cutlets with salt and pepper and sauté them on a very hot flame. Then combine them with the diced potatoes, pour over the onion sauce, adding 2 tablespoons of sour cream, and cook for a few minutes more.

Serves 4.

Lake Todos Los Santos, Chile

CHILE

EMPANADAS DE HORNO

YOU WILL NEED: onions, ground beef, shortening, paprika, salt, pepper, flour, beef broth, eggs, black olives, raisins.

Filling:

2 large onions, finely chopped
2 pounds finely ground beef
Shortening
1 tablespoon paprika
Salt and pepper
1 tablespoon flour
1 cup beef broth
3 hard-boiled eggs, sliced
16 black olives
1 cup raisins

Dough:

4 cups all-purpose flour
1 cup shortening
Salt
Water
2 eggs

The filling must be prepared the day before and allowed to set before filling the "Empanadas."

Fry the chopped onions and ground beef in a little shortening. Add the paprika, salt, and pepper. Add the flour and enough broth to make a thick gravy. Place in the refrigerator.

Sift the flour onto a board. Make a hole in the center. Melt the shortening, and allow it to cool slightly. Dissolve the salt in a cup of warm water. Beat the eggs slightly. Combine all the dough ingredients, and knead, adding water or flour as necessary for proper consistency.

Once the dough is soft and warm, lay it on the board and roll it thin, cutting from it individual pieces the size of a dinner plate. Into each piece of pastry, put a spoonful of filling, adding the raisins, olives, and slices of hard-boiled eggs. Wet the edges of the dough with a little water and fold it into a half moon shape. Seal the edges by rolling or pressing them together with a little water. Bake in a pre-heated oven (approximately 400 degrees) for about 30 minutes, or until golden brown.

Makes 16 Empanadas.

Castle at Lugh Leane, Ireland

IRELAND

DUBLIN CODDLE (Stew of Bacon and Sausage)

YOU WILL NEED: pork sausages, bacon, onions, potatoes, parsley, salt, pepper.

8 pork sausages
8 (¼ inch thick) **bacon slices**
1 quart (4 cups) **boiling water**
4 large onions, thinly sliced
2 pounds potatoes, peeled and sliced
4 tablespoons parsley, chopped
Salt and pepper to taste

Boil the sausages and bacon (cut both into large chunks) in the boiling water for 5 minutes. Drain, but reserve the liquid. Put the meat into a large saucepan (or an ovenproof dish) with the sliced onions and potatoes and the chopped parsley. Season to taste with salt and pepper and add enough of the reserved liquid to barely cover. Lay wax paper on top and then put on the lid and simmer gently, or cook in a slow to moderate oven, approximately 200 degrees, for about an hour, or until the liquid is reduced by half and all the ingredients are cooked but not mushy. Serve hot.

Serves 4.

Medieval town, Rothenburg, Germany

GERMANY

KALBSHAXE (Veal Shank)

YOU WILL NEED: carrots, onions, celery, salt, pepper, stock, veal, butter, bay leaf.

6 medium carrots, sliced
2 medium onions, sliced
2 stalks celery, chopped
Salt and pepper to taste
Water or stock
1 large (3 to 4 pounds) veal shank
3 tablespoons butter

Place the carrots, onions, celery, salt, and pepper in a large pot with just enough water or stock to cover. Cook the vegetables. When they're done, add the shank of veal and cook for 2½ to 3 hours over very low heat, adding more water when necessary. Remove the shank and brown it in hot butter until crisp.

Variation: Season the shank and fry it briefly with chopped onion in butter, turning now and then. Cover and cook over low heat for 2½ to 3 hours; add water as desired. Remove the shank. Blend together 1 tablespoon vinegar, 1 tablespoon flour, and water to make gravy. Pour the gravy over the shank to serve.

Serves 4.

Tivoli, Copenhagen, Denmark

Denmark

FLAESKESTEG MED RDKAL (Roast Ham with Red Cabbage)

YOU WILL NEED: ham, coarse salt, ginger, Gravy Master, potatoes, sugar, butter, pickled cucumber, red cabbage, red currant juice.

5 pounds ham
Coarse salt
1 teaspoon ginger
Boiling water
4 drops Gravy Master
3 tablespoons flour
Red Cabbage:
1 medium-sized red cabbage
2 tablespoons butter
6 tablespoons sugar
1½ pints red currant juice
Salt to taste

Caramelized Potatoes:
2 pounds very small potatoes
1¾ ounces sugar
1½ ounces butter
Seeded and pickled cucumber

Scrape the rind of the ham very carefully. Score it across the bone with a sharp knife in lines ½ inch apart. Or score it into squares. Dry the scored ham with a warm, slightly damp cloth. Rub the rind with coarse salt and a little ginger. Place the ham in a roasting tray in a hot oven. Allow it to cook for a few minutes, then pour over it a little boiling water. Allow the ham to cook for 3 hours, without basting. Half an hour before cooking is complete, strain off the gravy. Skim off any surplus fat. This gravy may be served as it stands, or thickened with creamed flour and butter. In either case, a few drops of Gravy Master should be added to give the sauce a nice color.

Red Cabbage: Shred the cabbage. Melt 2 heaping tablespoons of butter in a pan together with 6 heaping tablespoons of sugar. Cook gently, without allowing the mixture to brown. Add the cabbage. Stir carefully until the liquid evaporates. Gradually add the red currant juice, allowing the cabbage to absorb this liquid before adding more. Allow the cabbage to simmer for at least 3 hours. Finally, add salt to taste.

Caramelized Potatoes: Boil 2 pounds of potatoes. Peel them while they are still hot and rinse them in cold water. Cook 1¾ ounces of sugar in a pan. As soon as this begins to brown, add 1½ ounces of butter. Allow it to cook with the sugar. Add the potatoes and cook quickly, shaking the pan all the time.

Serves 6.

SAUDI ARABIA

KABSAH (Rice with Meat)

YOU WILL NEED: onions, butter, lamb, tomatoes, carrots, garlic, salt, black pepper, cardamom, rice.

4 onions, sliced
3 tablespoons butter
1 pound leg of lamb, cubed
6 tomatoes, sliced
2 carrots, sliced
2 cups water
1 teaspoon garlic, minced
Salt
1 teaspoon black pepper
1 teaspoon cardamom
4 cups rice

Brown the sliced onions in the butter. Add the meat cubes, tomatoes, carrots, water, garlic, salt, pepper, and cardamom. Cook over medium heat for approximately ½ hour, or until the meat is tender. Add the rice, and cook for another ¼ hour until the moisture (water) evaporates. Decrease the heat to low and continue to cook for another 10 minutes.

Serves 4.

Desert lake, Bandi Emir, Afghanistan

Afghanistan

NAURINJ OR ZARDA PALOW

YOU WILL NEED: fat, chicken, onion, salt, orange peel, sugar, blanched almonds, pistachios, saffron, rice, chicken broth, salt.

½ cup fat
1 medium chicken, whole or disjointed
1 large onion, sliced
2½ teaspoons salt
8 cups water
½ cup orange peel, cut into toothpick-sized strips
2½ cups sugar
½ cup blanched almonds, cut lengthwise
½ cup blanched pistachios
½ teaspoon saffron
2 cups long grain rice
2 quarts boiling water
3 cups chicken broth

Heat the fat in a kettle, and fry the chicken in the fat until it is lightly browned; add the onion, 1½ teaspoons of salt, and 6 cups of water, and simmer until the chicken is tender. Remove the chicken from the broth for the last steps of the cooking. Wash and cut up the orange peels;

Set aside. Make a syrup by bringing to a boil 2 cups of water and the sugar. Add to the boiling syrup the orange peel, almonds, and pistachios. Boil for 10 to 15 minutes. Strain and set aside the orange peel and nuts. Add the saffron to the syrup. Boil for 5 minutes. Set aside until the rice is cooked.

Cook the rice in the 2 quarts of boiling water with the remaining teaspoon of salt. Cook until tender. Drain and rinse the rice with cold water. While the rice is still in the strainer add to it the nuts and orange peel, reserving 3 to 4 tablespoons for garnish.

Pour the hot syrup over the rice, and into a kettle for further use. To complete the cooking and combine all the flavors, place ½ of the rice in a large casserole. Follow with the chicken, and top with the remaining rice. Mix the syrup with the chicken broth, and pour the mixture over the chicken and rice in the casserole. Cover and heat in a 300-degree oven for 20 to 30 minutes. All the liquid should be absorbed. To serve, place the chicken in the center of a large platter. Mound the rice mixture over the chicken and garnish with the orange peel and nuts reserved for that purpose.

Serves 6.

Shwedagon Pagoda, Rangoon

Burma

PRAWN AND BAMBOO SHOOT CURRY

YOU WILL NEED: prawns, bamboo shoots, garlic, onion, ginger, paprika, cooking oil, turmeric, salt, pepper.

½ pound prawns
1 pound bamboo shoots, sliced
¼ teaspoon garlic, ground
1 large onion, sliced
¼ teaspoon powdered ginger
¼ teaspoon paprika
2 tablespoons cooking oil
¼ teaspoon turmeric
Salt and pepper to taste

Fry the sliced onion in the cooking oil until golden brown. Add the turmeric, paprika, and a few spoonfuls of hot water. Simmer for a minute and add the garlic, ginger, salt, and pepper and fry. When the oil rises to the top of the spices, add the prawns and fry it until hardened. Then add the sliced bamboo shoots and enough water to cover them. Cook over medium heat until the bamboo shoots are tender. Do not let them get dry. Serve over rice.

Serves 2.

Punta Piedade, Portugal

Portugal

BACALHAU (Codfish, Portuguese Style)

YOU WILL NEED: eggs, potatoes, salt, cod, olive oil, garlic, onions, olives, seasoned salt, pepper, white wine, parsley.

4 eggs
4 medium potatoes
4 teaspoons salt
1½ pounds fresh cod fillets
½ cup olive oil
3 cloves garlic, peeled and finely chopped
3 medium onions, peeled and sliced
½ cup ripe pitted olives, chopped
½ teaspoon seasoned salt
⅛ teaspoon pepper
¼ cup white wine
Sprigs of parsley

Hard-boil the eggs well in advance, and keep them cool in cold water. Cook the potatoes in boiling water with a teaspoon of salt for about 20 minutes, or until tender. In a covered saucepan, over medium heat cook the codfish with 1 cup of water and 2 teaspoons of salt until tender.

Drain and peel the potatoes, cut them in half lengthwise, then cut them crosswise into ¼-inch-thick slices. Drain and flake the cod, removing the bones. Heat the oven to 350 degrees.

In a large skillet, heat the olive oil, add the garlic, onions, and potatoes, and brown well over medium heat, turning occasionally, for about 10 minutes. Add the olives, seasoned salt, and ½ teaspoon salt. Arrange half the mixture over the bottom of a 12 x 8 x 2 baking dish; evenly lay the cod over it; sprinkle the cod with ½ teaspoon salt and pepper. Cover with the rest of the potato mixture. Pour on the wine, then bake for 18 to 20 minutes, or until hot.

Shell the cold hard-boiled eggs, cut 2 of them into 4 wedges, chop the other 2 coarsely. Place 2 wedges and a sprig of parsley in each of the 4 corners of the baking dish. Sprinkle chopped eggs and snipped parsley along the center of the dish.
Serve immediately.

Serves 4.

St. Alexander Neosky Cathedral, Sofia, Bulgaria

GUVECH (Bulgarian Veal Stew)

YOU WILL NEED: onion, garlic, veal, cooking oil, potatoes, green peppers, eggplant, mushrooms, okra, carrots, green beans, green peas, tomatoes, grapes, salt, pepper, parsley, water.

1 large onion, cut into ¼-inch-thick slices
1 teaspoon garlic, coarsely chopped
3 pounds veal, cut into ½-inch cubes
1 cup mushrooms, sliced
4 to 6 potatoes, cut into 2-inch cubes
6 to 8 green peppers, cut into large pieces
1 eggplant, cut into 2-inch cubes
1 cup okra
3 medium-sized carrots, diced
1 cup green beans
4 medium-sized tomatoes, cut into cubes
¼ cup green peas
1 teaspoon salt
½ teaspoon black pepper
2 teaspoons parsley, chopped
1 cup cooking oil
2 cups water
¼ pound seeded grapes

Fry together the onions, garlic, and meat for 20 to 30 minutes in cooking oil. In separate pan fry the potatoes until brown, then add the green peppers, eggplant, and the other vegetables, except the tomatoes and grapes. Season this mixture with salt, pepper, and parsley. When the meat is fried well done apply water to steam and improve the quality of the meat. Pour off this water into a ceramic bowl and allow it to stand for 5 minutes, then add it to the vegetables. Mix together the vegetables and the meat and place the stew in a casserole dish. Add the tomatoes and bake for 45 minutes. Add the grapes and bake for another 15 minutes. Serve directly from the casserole.

To add a more exotic flavor to this dish, mix four eggs with 1 cup of yogurt and put the mixture on top of the stew before baking.

Serves 6.

Paramaribo, Surinam

KIPPENPASTEI (Chicken Pie)

YOU WILL NEED: flour, butter, chicken, onions, butter, bouillon cubes, salt, pepper, peas, carrots, capers, eggs.

Dough:

4 cups sifted all-purpose flour
½ pound cold butter
1 cup ice water

Filling:

1 3½-pound chicken, cut into pieces
1 cup onions, chopped
¼ cup butter
1 cup water
3 chicken bouillon cubes
2 teaspoons salt
¼ teaspoon pepper
1 10-ounce package frozen peas
2 cups fresh carrots, diced
2 tablespoons capers
4 hard-cooked eggs, sliced
1 egg white, slightly beaten

Place the sifted flour in a bowl, cut in the cold butter with a pastry blender until the mixture resembles coarse meal. Add the ice water all at once, and blend to form the dough. Roll out the dough, repeat several times, form it into a ball again, and let it stand for 10 to 15 minutes. Divide the dough in half, roll one half into a 14-inch circle, about ¼ inch thick. Fit the pastry into a 10-inch pie pan, patting out any air bubbles. Trim the overhang to ½ inch. Roll the remaining half of the dough into another 14-inch circle, and cut it into ½-inch strips; reserve the strips for the lattice top on the pie.

Wash and dry the chicken. Place the butter in a frying pan, and sauté the chicken and onions until they're golden brown. Add the water and bouillon cubes, and simmer until the chicken is tender. Remove the chicken from the bones, cut the meat into 1-inch pieces, and return it to the frying pan. Add the salt, pepper, peas, carrots, capers, and simmer for 15 minutes.

Spoon the chicken mixture into a pastry-lined pan, using a slotted spoon. Place the hard-cooked egg slices over the top of the pie; place the pastry strips over the pie to make a lattice top, flute the edges, and brush the pastry with egg white. Bake for 40 minutes at 375 degrees, or until golden brown. Serves 6.

Suzdal Rozhdestvensky Cathedral, USSR

RUSSIA

BEEF STROGANOFF

YOU WILL NEED: butter, flour, beef stock or condensed consommé, mustard, tomato paste, onion, mushrooms, beef, salt, pepper, sour cream, potatoes.

3 tablespoons butter
1½ tablespoons flour
2 cups beef stock or condensed consommé
1 teaspoon prepared mustard
2 tablespoons tomato paste
1 medium onion, chopped
½ pound fresh mushrooms, sliced
2 pounds fillet of beef, cut into thin strips 2 inches long and ½ inch wide
1½ teaspoons salt
½ teaspoon pepper
¼ cup sour cream
24 small potatoes, boiled

In a saucepan melt 1 tablespoon of butter, and brown the flour lightly; then stir in the beef stock, mustard, and tomato paste. Bring to a boil and cook until thickened. Set aside.

In a large skillet melt 2 tablespoons of butter, and sauté the onion and mushrooms until golden. Add the beef and brown, stirring frequently. Stir in salt and pepper, then the sauce. Simmer, covered, for about 20 minutes, or until the meat is tender.

In a small bowl beat the sour cream and part of the sauce from the skillet. Add the mixture to the meat in the skillet. Heat gently. Serve with small boiled potatoes.

Serves 4

Bali Tampaksiring Sanctuary, Indonesia

Indonesia

SATE (Lamb Skiskebab)

YOU WILL NEED: lamb, vinegar, garlic, peanut butter, milk, bouillon broth, red pepper, soy sauce, sugar, bay leaf, salt.

3 cups lamb, cut into 1½-inch cubes
½ teaspoon vinegar
¼ teaspoon garlic, chopped
½ cup water

Put 5 cubes of meat on each skewer. Mix together the other ingredients and dip the meat into the mixture. Bake in preheated oven at 300 to 350 degrees for 30 minutes. Serve with hot sauce.

Sauce:
4 tablespoons peanut butter
½ teaspoon garlic, chopped
½ cup milk
½ cup bouillon broth
1 teaspoon ground red pepper
1 teaspoon soy sauce
1 teaspoon sugar
1 bay leaf
Salt to taste

Combine all the ingredients and cook over low heat, stirring continuously. When the sauce is thickened, remove it from the heat.

Serves 4.

Bay of Biscay, Ondarroa, Spain

SPAIN

PAELLA A LA VALENCIANA

YOU WILL NEED: veal, pork, chicken, olive oil, garlic, onion, tomatoes, rice, clams, red peppers, crab meat, peas, lobster, artichoke hearts, saffron, garlic, salt, pepper.

½ pound veal, cubed
½ pound pork, cubed
2 chickens, cut into frying pieces
½ cup olive oil
2 cloves garlic, crushed
1 large onion, finely cut
2 pounds tomatoes, peeled
4 cups rice
2 cups water
20 clams in shell
2 sweet red peppers, cut into chunks
1 pound crab meat
2 packages frozen peas
1 pound lobster meat
10 artichoke hearts
2 tablespoons saffron powder
2 cloves garlic, mashed
Salt and pepper to taste

Brown the veal, pork, and chicken in the olive oil with the first 2 cloves of garlic and the cut onion. Add the tomatoes and cook for 10 minutes at a simmer. Place the following ingredients in a large casserole: the rice and water, clams, red peppers, crab meat, frozen peas, lobster meat, and artichoke hearts. Make a paste of the saffron powder and the other 2 cloves of garlic and stir it into the rice. Cook, covered, in 350-degree oven for 10 minutes. Remove the cover, and cook for 10 minutes longer.

Serves 10.

Camel Corps, Jordan

JORDAN

WARAK INIB MIHSHEE (Grape Leaf Rolls)

YOU WILL NEED: grape leaves, lemons, lamb bones, rice, lamb, salt, pepper.

50 Grape leaves
1 teaspoon salt
Juice of 2 lemons
4 lamb bones

Soak fresh grape leaves in hot water for 15 minutes to soften. Remove from water, squeeze out moisture, and stem each leaf. Place 1 tablespoon of stuffing across each leaf, fold end of leaf like an envelope, and roll away from you. Place lamb bones on bottom of pan. Arrange stuffed leaves in rows in pan, alternating direction of each row. Sprinkle salt over stuffed leaves. Press leaves down with inverted dish. Add water to reach dish. Cover pan and cook on low fire for 35 minutes until tender. During last 10 minutes of cooking, add lemon juice.

Serves 6.

Stuffing
1 cup rice, rinsed in water
1 pound lamb or beef, fat and lean, chopped fine
Salt and pepper to taste

Combine all ingredients, mix well, and set aside.

Berber Dancers, Goulimime, Morocco

MOROCCO

DJAJ M'KALLI
(Chicken with Lemon and Olives)

YOU WILL NEED: chicken, garlic, salt, vegetable oil, ginger, turmeric, black pepper, saffron, salt, onions, butter, garlic, Greek Kalamata olives, pickled lemons*.

3 chickens, halved
6 to 8 cloves garlic, crushed
About 2 tablespoons salt
¾ cup vegetable oil
2 teaspoons ginger
1 teaspoon turmeric
1 teaspoon black pepper
Pinch of saffron
3 medium onions, grated
1 stick butter
2 to 3 cloves garlic, chopped
About 1 quart water
½ jar Greek Kalamata olives
2 pickled lemons*

Rub the chickens with the crushed garlic and salt, and put them in a large pot with water to cover. Let stand for 1 hour, then remove the chickens from the water. Rub the chickens with a mixture of the vegetable oil, ginger, turmeric, black pepper, saffron, and salt to taste. Allow the chickens to marinate for a few hours or overnight in the refrigerator. Place the chickens in a pot and add the grated onions, butter, chopped garlic, and a quart of water. Bring the water to a boil, then simmer until the chickens are tender. When they're almost done, add the Greek olives and the pickled lemons*. (Be sure to wash the brine off the lemons.) When the chickens are done, remove them from the pot and boil down the sauce until it is fairly thick. Return the chickens to the sauce and reheat before serving.

**Pickled lemons:* Quarter the lemons leaving one end attached. Fill them with salt and put them in a glass or stoneware jar with a tight lid. Put in as many lemons as will fit the jar snugly. Let stand for at least 2 weeks.

Serves 8.

Positano, Italy

ITALY

SPAGHETTI ALLA MOLISANA

YOU WILL NEED: onion, butter, Prosciutto, parsley, basil, red pepper, garlic, oregano, salt, tomatoes, spaghetti, Romano cheese.

- **2 thin slices** (large) **onion**
- **¼ pound butter**
- **½ pound Prosciutto, diced**
- **2 teaspoons parsley**
- **½ teaspoon basil**
- **¼ teaspoon red pepper**
- **1 clove garlic, chopped**
- **¼ teaspoon oregano**
- **½ teaspoon salt**
- **2 pounds peeled tomatoes**
- **1 pound spaghetti**
- **4 tablespoons Romano cheese**

Simmer the onion slices in butter until golden. Add the Prosciutto, parsley, basil, red pepper, chopped garlic, oregano, and salt. Cook for a few minutes and then add the peeled tomatoes. Cook for 40 minutes.

Boil the spaghetti in salted water for about 12 minutes *(al dente).* Drain, and place it on a warm serving dish. Add the sauce and toss the spaghetti. Sprinkle with Romano cheese.

Serves 4.

Farm Village in the Tatra Mountains, Czechoslovakia

CZECHOSLOVAKIA

PORK CHOPS A LA BRATISLAVA

YOU WILL NEED: pork chops, salt, pepper, shortening, green peppers, onion, tomatoes, caraway seeds, butter.

8 pork chops
Salt and pepper to taste
Shortening
2 large green peppers
1 large onion
2 large tomatoes
1 teaspoon caraway seeds
½ tablespoon butter

Tenderize the chops by pounding and season them with salt and pepper. Fry the chops in a small amount of shortening. Finely slice the peppers, onion, and tomatoes, and sauté them with caraway seeds in a separate pan with butter. When the pork chops are well done, serve them with the vegetables and boiled potatoes.

Serves 4.

Pont Alexandre, Paris

France

GIGOT D'AGNEAU AUX MARRONS
(Leg of Lamb with Chestnuts)

YOU WILL NEED: lamb, salt, pepper, flour, chestnut puree, onions, chicken broth, white wine, bread crumbs, butter.

1 5- to 6-pound leg of lamb
Salt and pepper
Flour
1 10-ounce can French unsweetened chestnut puree
4 medium onions, sliced
½ cup chicken broth
½ cup white wine
1 cup bread crumbs
Butter

Have the lamb boned and tied with twine to reshape it. Sprinkle it with salt and pepper, and dust it with flour. Roast it in a 350-degree oven for about 2 hours. Meanwhile combine the onions, broth, and wine. Simmer until the onions are soft. Drain, reserving the cooking liquid. Puree the onions in a sieve or blender. Heat the chestnut puree, and blend in the onion puree.

When the lamb is cooked, remove it from the oven, and let it rest for 15 minutes. Slice the lamb but do not cut through, and do not dislodge the slices. Spread the combined purees between the slices, reshape the meat, and tie it together to keep its shape. Moisten with the reserved cooking liquid, cover with bread crumbs, and dot with butter. Increase oven heat to 400 degrees; toast the lamb for another 15 to 20 minutes.

Serves 6.

Inca ruins of Macchu-Picchu, Peru

PERU

ARROZ CON PATO (Rice with Duck)

YOU WILL NEED: duck, pork, lard, onion, tomatoes, garlic, salt, parsley, chili powder, rice, peas, brandy.

1 duck, cut into serving pieces
1 pound pork cutlets
2 tablespoons lard
1 large onion, chopped
1½ cups stewed tomatoes
2 cloves garlic, mashed
1 teaspoon salt
2 tablespoons parsley, finely minced
1 tablespoon chili powder
1 pound rice
1 package frozen peas
¼ cup brandy

Brown the duck and pork in the lard, add the onion, tomatoes, garlic, salt, parsley, and chili powder, and mix well. Add water to just cover the stew, and cook until the duck is tender, about 1 hour. Add the rice and continue cooking for 20 minutes. Add the frozen peas and cook for 10 minutes longer. If necessary, during the process add more water, but be cautious, as it should all be absorbed by the time the dish is finished. Remove the pork. Add the brandy and serve at once.

Serves 4.

Castle Combe, England

ENGLAND

YORKSHIRE BEEF HOTPOT

YOU WILL NEED: stewing beef, flour, salt, oil, onion, Bovril, potatoes, Lancashire cheese (optional).

1½ pounds stewing beef
1 tablespoon flour
½ teaspoon salt
2 tablespoons oil
1 onion, sliced
1 teaspoon Bovril
1 cup water
2 potatoes, peeled and sliced
Crumbled Lancashire cheese (optional)

Rub the beef with a mixture of the flour and the salt. Brown the beef in oil, a few pieces at a time. Lay the browned beef and the raw onion slices in a casserole. Mix the Bovril with water and pour the mixture over the beef. Arrange the potatoes in overlapping slices on top of the beef. Place the casserole in a 250-degree oven and let it cook for 2 hours. If the potatoes get too crisp cover the dish. Soft and crumbly Lancashire cheese is often sprinkled over the potatoes for the last 5 minutes of cooking time, or after removing the casserole from the oven.

Serves 4.

Caracas, Venezuela

Venezuela

HALLACAS (Corn Pie)

YOU WILL NEED: white cornmeal, butter, eggs, salt, chicken, pork, tomatoes, onion, parsley, garlic, capers, olives, raisins, cayenne pepper, black pepper, oregano, allspice, chilies.

Dough:

1½ pounds white corn meal
2½ pints boiling salt water
8 ounces butter
2 eggs

Stuffing:

1 3-pound roasting chicken
2 pounds pork
1 pound tomatoes
1 large onion, chopped
3 tablespoons parsley, chopped
1 clove garlic, crushed
1 tablespoon capers
1 cup whole olives
1 cup raisins
Pinch of cayenne pepper
Pinch of black pepper
Pinch of oregano
Pinch of allspice
½ teaspoon crushed dried chilies
Boiling salt water

Pour the cornmeal into rapidly boiling salt water. Add the butter and cook for approximately 8 to 10 minutes, stirring. Add lightly beaten eggs and blend to form dough. Divide the dough into quarters and then cut each quarter into 5 portions, making portions into 6-inch squares.

Simmer the chicken and pork in water until almost tender. Remove the bones and cut the meat into small pieces. Return the meat to the water, add the tomatoes, onion, parsley, garlic, capers, olives, raisins, both peppers, oregano, allspice, and chilies and simmer for about 1 hour, stirring occasionally.

Place 2 or 3 tablespoons of stuffing on one side of the dough and fold over the other side, like a pie. Wrap cooking paper or foil securely around the squares. Tie crosswise with a string to secure the "package" firmly. Boil for about 2 hours in boiling salt water to cover. Serve piping hot. Only those Hallacas which are to be consumed at once may be unwrapped. Keep the others in their original wrappings in the refrigerator. Do not freeze. Heat them in boiling salt water when ready to be eaten.

Makes 20 to 24 Hallacas.

Middle Point Cove, Halifax, Nova Scotia

CANADA

NOVA SCOTIA FISH CHOWDER

YOU WILL NEED: halibut, cod, or haddock; salt pork; onion; potatoes; milk; evaporated milk; soda crackers; butter; parsley; salt; pepper.

2 pounds halibut, cod, or haddock fillets
¼ pound fat salt pork, diced
1 medium onion, chopped
2 cups potatoes, diced
2 cups water
1 quart fresh milk
⅔ cup evaporated milk
8 soda crackers, crushed
3 tablespoons butter
2 tablespoons parsley, chopped
2 teaspoons salt
⅛ teaspoon pepper

Cut the fish into bite-sized chunks. Sauté the salt pork until it is a delicate brown. Save the scraps for garnish.

Sauté the onions until tender, add the potatoes and water and simmer until the potatoes are just cooked, then add the fish and simmer for 5 minutes. Combine the remaining ingredients and heat but don't boil. Add this mixture to the fish mixture and serve piping hot. Garnish with the pork scraps.

Serves 8.

Buenos Aires, Argentina

CARBONADA CRIOLLA II

YOU WILL NEED: garlic, butter, onion, tomatoes, green pepper, beef, salt, sugar, peaches, potatoes, sweet potatoes, corn, beef broth, pumpkin, pepper, butter.

2 cloves garlic
3 tablespoons butter
1 large onion, chopped
2 tomatoes, coarsely chopped
1 green pepper, chopped
1½ pounds tender beef, cubed
Salt
1 cube sugar
4 peaches, peeled and halved
3 potatoes, diced
3 sweet potatoes, diced
6 ears of corn, kernels cut from cob (not grated)
1½ cups beef broth
1 pumpkin
Pepper
Butter

Fry the garlic in the butter. When it is well browned remove and discard it; add the chopped onion, fry it for a few minutes, then add the tomatoes, pepper, beef, salt, and sugar. Let cook for 15 minutes and add the peaches and potatoes. Stir, lower the heat, and add the corn and beef broth. Simmer for 40 minutes, adding more broth if the mixture becomes too dry. Meanwhile cut off the top of the pumpkin and scoop out the seeds and membranes; salt and pepper the inside well and butter the edge. Then bake the pumpkin until somewhat browned but not too soft. When the Carbonada is ready, fill the pumpkin with it and serve hot directly from the pumpkin.

Serves 6.

St. Moritz, Switzerland

Switzerland

FONDUE SUPREME

YOU WILL NEED: Swiss cheese, Gruyère cheese, garlic, white wine, lemon juice, nutmeg, cornstarch, Kirsch, Italian or French bread, champagne, apples, pears, melon, grapes.

1 clove fresh garlic
1 cup dry white wine
1 tablespoon lemon juice
½ pound shredded Swiss cheese (Shred cheese in advance and store in tightly closed plastic bag in refrigerator)
½ pound shredded natural Gruyère cheese (Treat same as Swiss cheese)
Nutmeg to taste
1 tablespoon cornstarch
3 tablespoons Kirsch
2 loaves Italian or French bread (cut into 1-inch cubes with crust on one side)
⅓ cup champagne
Assorted fruits for dunking: apple and pear slices, melon, grapes.

Rub the cooking pot with cut garlic; add the wine and heat. When the wine is hot, not boiling, add the lemon juice. Add the shredded cheese by handfuls, stirring constantly with a wooden fork or spoon until the cheese is smooth and melted. Bring the fondue to a bubble briefly. Add the nutmeg and stir until blended. Mix the cornstarch with the Kirsch. Add to the fondue and allow it to boil for another 15 to 30 seconds. Add the champagne. Serve and keep hot over burner. Spear the bread cubes (through soft side into crust) and the fruits for dunking, and swirl them in the fondue. Serve with dry white wine.

Serves 4.

Rio de Janeiro, Brazil

Brazil

GALINHA COM RECHEIO DE CASTANHA (Chicken with Chestnut Dressing)

YOU WILL NEED: chicken, white wine, garlic, lemon, salt, chives, parsley, giblets, butter, pepper, nutmeg, chestnut purée, bacon.

5 pound roasting chicken
¾ pint white wine
1 clove garlic, crushed
Juice of 1 lemon
1½ teaspoons salt
1 teaspoon chives, chopped
1 tablespoon parsley, finely chopped
Giblets, chopped
1 tablespoon butter
Pinch of pepper
Pinch of nutmeg
8 ounces chestnut purée
5 slices bacon

Marinate the chicken in a mixture of the wine, garlic, lemon juice, ¾ teaspoon salt, chives, and parsley, and place in the refrigerator for 24 hours. Drain and wipe the chicken dry.

Cook the giblets in the butter; add the pepper, nutmeg, chestnut purée, and ¾ teaspoon salt. Place the mixture inside the chicken; arrange the slices of bacon over the breast of the chicken. Wrap the chicken in foil and place it in a roasting tine, breast side up. Cook it for 2 hours in a moderate oven, 375 degrees. When nearly done open the foil to brown the chicken.

Serves 4.

Carnival, Trinidad

FRUITS DE MER A LA TRINIDAD

YOU WILL NEED: shrimp, lobster, snapper, oysters, mushrooms, onion, salt, Tabasco sauce, sherry wine, butter, flour, milk, Parmesan cheese, potatoes.

½ cup raw shrimp, chopped
½ cup raw lobster meat, chopped
½ cup raw snapper, chopped
½ cup raw oysters, chopped
½ cup mushrooms, chopped
¼ cup onion, chopped
1 teaspoon salt
¾ teaspoon Tabasco sauce
1 cup sherry wine
½ cup butter
1 cup flour
1 quart milk
¼ cup Parmesan cheese, grated
3 cups Duchess potatoes (6 medium potatoes, cooked, mashed, with 1 egg added) lengthwise

Bring to a boil the shrimp, lobster, snapper, oysters, mushrooms, onion, salt, and Tabasco sauce in the sherry wine; cook for 10 minutes. Remove the ingredients from the stock and keep them hot. Melt the butter, blend in the flour, and gradually add the milk; cook over low heat until the sauce thickens, stirring frequently. Add the fish mixture and 2 tablespoons of the Parmesan cheese to the white sauce. Spoon the mixture into 6 individual casseroles; using a pastry tube garnish the edges with the Duchess potatoes, and sprinkle the tops with the remaining Parmesan cheese. Place the casseroles on a baking sheet and place them under the broiler for a few minutes to brown the potatoes lightly.

Serves 6.

VINAIGRETTE SAUCE (for above dish)

YOU WILL NEED: vinegar, olive oil, salt, dry mustard, pepper, parsley, onion, Tabasco sauce.

⅓ cup vinegar
¾ cup olive oil
2 teaspoons salt
2 teaspoons dry mustard
¼ teaspoon pepper
1 tablespoon parsley, chopped
1 tablespoon onion, chopped
Dash of Tabasco sauce

Combine the vinegar, olive oil, salt, dry mustard, pepper, parsley, onion, Tabasco sauce, and blend well.

The Rosary Quay, Bruges, Belgium

Belgium

POISSON A L'OSTENDAISE

YOU WILL NEED: halibut, mussels, mushrooms, shrimp, thyme, onion, carrot, parsley, bay leaf, butter, flour, Gruyère cheese, egg yolks, heavy cream, salt, pepper.

4 halibut steaks
½ cup shelled mussels, cooked
1 cup mushrooms
½ cup shelled shrimp, cooked and diced
1 teaspoon thyme
1 small onion
1 carrot
Parsley
1 bay leaf
1 tablespoon butter
3 tablespoons flour
¼ cup Gruyere cheese, grated
2 egg yolks
¼ cup heavy cream
6 cups water
1 tablespoon salt
Pepper to taste

Prepare a court bouillon made with water, salt, thyme, onion, carrot, parsley, and bay leaf.

Poach the fish steaks in the boiling bouillon, bringing the liquid to a second boil and then reducing the heat for 10 minutes. Remove the fish, drain; skin the fish and discard the bones. Keep the fish steaks warm.

Melt the butter in saucepan and stir in the flour. When the mixture is well blended, slowly add 3 cups of the fish bouillon. Add the Gruyère cheese and allow it to melt. Then add the egg yolks, stirring well, and also the heavy cream. Be careful not to let the sauce boil.

Boil the mushrooms for 2 minutes in a little of the remaining bouillon. Drain. Now add to the sauce the mushrooms, shrimp, and mussels. Season to taste with salt and pepper.

Arrange the fish steaks in a buttered oven dish and pour the sauce over them. Place the dish under a broiler until the sauce is golden brown.

Serves 4.

Pearl River, Kwangtung Province, China

SWEET AND SOUR PORK

YOU WILL NEED: pork, salt, pepper, sesame oil, sherry, cornstarch, peanut oil, egg, water, sugar, malt vinegar, tomato ketchup, pineapple cubes, red chili pepper, green peppers, pickled cabbage, carrot, cucumber.

½ pound lean leg of pork, cut into 1-inch cubes
Pinch of salt, pepper
½ teaspoon sesame oil
½ teaspoon sherry
1 tablespoon cornstarch
Peanut oil for deep frying

Batter:
3 ounces cornstarch
1 small egg
⅔ cup water
½ teaspoon peanut oil

Sweet and Sour Sauce:
⅔ cup water
¾ tablespoon sugar
¾ tablespoon cornstarch
Tiny pinch of salt, pepper
½ teaspoon tomato ketchup
1½ to 2 tablespoons malt vinegar
1 pound pineapple cubes
One red chili pepper
Green peppers to taste

Vegetable Garnish:
1 tablespoon each pickled cabbage, carrot, and cucumber. To make the batter: Sift the cornstarch into a pan. Make a well in the center, drop in the egg, then gradually add water and beat the mixture. Finally, stir in the oil. Set aside for 20 minutes.

To make the sweet and sour sauce: Bring the water with sugar, salt, pepper, ketchup, and vinegar to a boil. Stir in the cornstarch blended with a little water and cook for 1 to 1½ minutes. Lightly fry the pineapple, chopped chili, and green peppers for 1 minute. Stir briskly while frying. Add to the sweet and sour sauce. Keep hot.

To prepare the pork: Place the pork in a bowl. Add the seasonings, sesame oil, and sherry, and work them well into the pork. Coat the diced pork with flour. Turn the cubes into a sieve and toss about to shake off the excess flour. Drop the meat into the batter. As the pork has to be cooked thoroughly, have the peanut oil pre-heated to 360 degrees. Drop the pork into it, raise the heat, and cook the pork for 8 to 9 minutes until it is a warm golden color. Drain and dry on absorbent paper.

Turn the pork into a heated serving dish, deep enough to contain all the ingredients. Then add the pickled vegetables and spoon the sweet and sour sauce over them.

Serves 4.

Rumeli Fortress, Turkey

Turkey

TURLU (Vegetable Pot)

YOU WILL NEED: onions, butter, lamb, tomatoes, zucchini, eggplant, okra, green peppers, salt and pepper, green beans.

2 medium onions, chopped
¼ cup butter
1 pound lamb, diced
1½ cups water
3 medium tomatoes
2 small zucchini
1 medium eggplant
¼ pound okra
2 large green peppers
½ pound green beans
Salt and pepper to taste

Sauté the onions in the butter in a large saucepan until lightly browned. Add the meat and ½ cup of water, and simmer until the meat is nearly tender. While the meat is cooking, prepare the vegetables as follows: peel and slice the tomatoes and the zucchini. Peel 1-inch strips of skin from the eggplant and cut the eggplant into 2-inch segments. Trim the okra by removing the cone-shaped portions at the top. Remove the seeds from the green peppers and dice the peppers. When the meat is nearly tender, add 1 cup of hot water, salt, and pepper; then add the beans, zucchini, eggplant, tomatoes, pepper, and okra in that order. Cover the pan tightly and cook until the vegetables are done, about 50 minutes. If necessary, hot water may be added during cooking.

Serves 2.

Thai classical dancing, Bangkok

THAILAND

BEEF MUSSULMAN CURRY

YOU WILL NEED: beef, coconut cream*, peanuts, nam pia, curry paste, cinnamon, cardamom, tamarind pods, lime, palm sugar.

2 to 2½ pounds beef
4 cups coconut cream*
1 cup unsalted peanuts
Nam pia to taste (obtained in Chinese markets as shrimp sauce or paste, or substitute soy sauce with a touch of anchovy paste)
½-inch stick of cinnamon
15 cardamom seeds
Pulp from 3 tamarind pods (obtained from Spanish markets)
Juice of 1 lime
Palm sugar to taste (obtained in Spanish markets, or substitute light brown sugar)
1 tablespoon curry paste

Cut the beef into 2-inch cubes. Simmer in a covered saucepan with the coconut cream, peanuts, and nam pia until tender. Remove the meat and reduce the cream by one-third. Stir in the curry paste. Add the meat, cinnamon, and cardamom, cover and simmer until you have a smooth, slightly thickened consistency. Season with nam pia, tamarind, lime juice, and sugar to taste. Serve over steamed or fried long grain white rice with a side dish of finely minced raw red or green chili peppers.

**Coconut Cream:* To make 4 cups of coconut cream, pour 3 cups of boiling water over the grated meat of 1 coconut which has been tied tightly in a double piece of cheesecloth and placed in a deep bowl. Squeeze the water through the bag of coconut meat several times, each time wringing all the liquid out of the bag before repouring. The result is coconut cream. To grate the coconut easily, put a few pieces at a time in a blender on low speed.

Serves 4.

Marinduque, Philippines

Philippine Islands

CHICKEN AND PORK ADOBO
(Braised Chicken and Pork)

YOU WILL NEED: chicken, pork, vinegar, garlic, soy sauce, salt, pepper, lard.

1 1½-pound chicken, cut into 6 to 8 pieces (reserve liver)
2 pounds pork, cut with considerable fat into 1-inch cubes
½ cup vinegar
4 cloves garlic
2 tablespoons soy sauce
½ teaspoon salt
¼ teaspoon pepper
2 tablespoons lard

Place the chicken and pork in a saucepan and add the vinegar, garlic, soy sauce, salt, and pepper. Bring to a boil and simmer until the meat is tender, approximately 45 minutes. Remove the meat and drain, reserving the liquid. Sauté the meat in the lard in a skillet until well browned. Strain the liquid that has been reserved and return it to the saucepan.

Meanwhile, mash or grind the liver of the chicken and add it to the liquid in the saucepan. Add the browned meat to the liquid and mix carefully to avoid breaking up the meat. Add more salt and pepper if needed. Keep hot until ready. Serve with boiled rice.

Serves 6.

Canals, Amsterdam, Holland

HOLLAND

RUNDERLAPPEN (Pickled Steaks)

YOU WILL NEED: round steak, salt, pepper, butter or oil, onions, wine vinegar, mustard, bay leaf, cloves, peppercorns.

2 pounds round steak, cut into 4 slices
Salt and freshly ground pepper
1 stick butter, or 8 tablespoons oil
2 medium onions, sliced
2 tablespoons wine vinegar
2 teaspoons prepared mustard
½ cup water
1 bay leaf
5 cloves
5 peppercorns

Scrape the meat and rub it with salt and pepper. Heat the butter or oil, and brown the meat thoroughly on both sides. On lowered heat, add the onions and fry them until they are transparent. Mix the vinegar and mustard, add the water, and pour this over the meat, scraping the bottom of the skillet to loosen any particles. Add the cloves and peppercorns. Cover and simmer for about 2 hours, or until very tender, turning the meat every half hour. (If desired, strain the sauce and thicken with a little flour just before serving.)

Serves 4.

Jaipur, India

CHILLI CHICKEN

YOU WILL NEED: chicken, salt, red pepper, black pepper, eggs, flour, white mushrooms, salad oil, cucumber, spring onion, garlic, ginger, chilli peppers, vinegar, stock, sherry, sugar, soya-bean sauce, Ve-Tsin, white pepper.

1 to 1½ pounds chicken, diced
2 teaspoons salt
¼ teaspoon red pepper
¼ teaspoon black pepper
2 egg whites
½ ounce flour
1 ounce white mushrooms
4 ounces salad oil
½ pound cucumber
1 spring onion
6 cloves garlic
½ ounce ginger
6 green chilli peppers

Sauce:
1 tablespoon vinegar
3 tablespoons stock prepared from neck and gizzard of chicken
¾ tablespoon sherry
1 heaping tablespoon flour
½ teaspoon salt
1 teaspoon sugar
¾ tablespoon soya-bean sauce
1 teaspoon Ve-Tsin (Chinese flavoring)
½ teaspoon white pepper

Clean the chicken, remove the skin and bones and wash. Cut it into 12 pieces. Dip each piece into a mixture of 1 teaspoon of salt, red pepper, and black pepper, egg whites, and flour.

Having soaked the mushrooms overnight, boil them in the same water for 15 to 20 minutes. Heat 2 ounces of the salad oil in a skillet and fry a few pieces of the chicken at a time for 4 to 5 minutes, or until all of them are done. Remove the pieces from the oil and put them aside. Dice the cucumber, add a little salt, and leave it for 15 to 20 minutes. Then squeeze out the water. Heat the remaining 2 ounces of oil, and fry the finely chopped onion, garlic, ginger, mushrooms, chili peppers, and cucumber all separately, adding a pinch of salt to each. When all are fried, combine them in the skillet, and add the fried chicken and all the ingredients for the sauce mixed together. Cook for about 5 minutes. Serve hot over boiled rice.

Serves 4.

Gripsholm Castle, Lake Malar, Sweden

SWEDEN

PLOMMONSPACKAD FLASKKARRE
(Loin of Pork with Prunes)

YOU WILL NEED: prunes, pork, salt, pepper, ginger.

10 prunes, halved and pitted
½ cup warm water
4 pounds loin of pork
2 teaspoons salt
½ teaspoon pepper
¼ teaspoon ginger

Soak the halved prunes in the warm water for about ½ hour. Drain, saving the liquid. Insert the prunes deeply into the meat. Rub the meat with the salt, pepper, and ginger. Tie the roast into shape with a string. Place it in a small roasting pan and roast, uncovered, in a slow oven, 325 degrees for 40 to 45 minutes per pound. Remove the roast to a hot serving platter; remove the string and cut away the backbone. Add the prune juice to the drippings in the pan and cook, stirring, for a few minutes. Strain the liquid and serve it as gravy.

Serves 6.

Yukon Canyon, Mexico

MEXICO

CHICKEN MOLE

YOU WILL NEED: butter, chicken, salt, chicken broth, green pepper, sesame seeds, garlic, cloves, cinnamon, pepper, coriander, unsweetened chocolate, almonds, chili powder, tomatoes, rice, pimentos.

Butter
2½ pound fryer chicken, cut up
1 teaspoon salt
1½ cups canned chicken broth
1 green pepper, seeded
1 tablespoon sesame seeds
4 cloves garlic
Pinch of powdered cloves
¼ teaspoon cinnamon
Pinch of pepper
¼ teaspoon whole coriander
1 square unsweetened chocolate, grated
⅓ cup almonds, ground
1½ tablespoons chili powder
3 large tomatoes, peeled
4 cups hot cooked rice
2 pimentos, quartered

Melt the butter in a large skillet, and brown the chicken well on all sides, a few pieces at a time; add butter as needed. Remove the browned chicken to a 3-quart casserole, and sprinkle the pieces with salt to taste. Heat the oven to 375 degrees.

In a blender combine 1 teaspoon of salt, ½ cup of chicken broth, green pepper, sesame seeds, garlic, cloves, cinnamon, pepper, coriander, chocolate, almonds, chili powder, and tomatoes, and blend until well combined.

In the skillet in which the chicken was browned, combine the sauce with 1 cup of chicken broth; simmer, stirring, for 10 to 12 minutes; pour the sauce over the chicken. Bake, covered, for about 1½ to 1¾ hours. Serve with rice tossed with pimentos.

Serves 6.

Midnight sunset above the Arctic Circle, Finland

Finland

KESAEKEITTO (Summer Vegetable Soup)

YOU WILL NEED: carrots, potatoes, peas, cauliflower, spinach, sugar, nutmeg, salt, flour, milk, prawns, parsley.

1 cup raw carrots, sliced
1 cup raw potatoes, diced
1 pound fresh peas, shelled
1 cup raw cauliflower
½ cup fresh spinach, chopped
1½ tablespoons sugar
1½ tablespoons nutmeg
2 teaspoons salt
2 tablespoons flour
1 pint water
2 pints milk
6 ounces prawns, cooked and deveined
Parsley, snipped

Clean the vegetables and cut them into pieces. Place all but the spinach in salted water. Add the sugar and nutmeg and bring the water to a boil. Cook for about 30 to 40 minutes. Add the spinach and simmer for 10 minutes longer. Warm the milk. Melt the butter, stir in the flour, cook them well together, and gradually mix in the warmed milk. Add the vegetables wtih their stock and the prawns. Pour the soup into a tureen and sprinkle with parsley.

Serves 6.

Cape Town Camp Bay, South Africa

South Africa

BOBOTIE

YOU WILL NEED: onions, apple, butter, lamb, beef, bread, curry powder, sugar, eggs, vinegar, salt, pepper, raisins, almonds, bay leaves, milk, turmeric (optional).

2 onions, finely sliced
1 apple, diced
2 tablespoons butter
2 pounds meat (half lamb and half beef), **cooked and minced**
2 slices bread, soaked and squeezed out
2 tablespoons curry powder
2 tablespoons sugar
2 eggs
2 tablespoons vinegar
2 teaspoons salt
¼ teaspoon pepper
¼ cup raisins
12 almonds
6 bay leaves
1 cup milk

Fry the onion and apple in the butter and mix with the meat, bread, curry, sugar, 1 egg, vinegar, salt, pepper, and raisins. Blanch and remove the skins of the almonds, cut the almonds into quarters, and add. Mix well. Place the mixture in a greased baking dish. Arrange the bay leaves in the meat with half of the leaves inside and half sticking out above the meat. Bake in 350-degree oven for 30 to 45 minutes, until the custard is set. Beat the second egg with the milk and pour it over the Bobotie about 10 minutes before it is removed from the oven. Serve with rice and chutney.

Serves 8.

San Pablo, Ecuador

ECUADOR

SEAFOOD IN PICKLE SAUCE

YOU WILL NEED: shrimp, onion, lemons, olive oil, white vinegar, salt, pepper, Worcestershire sauce, Tabasco sauce, prepared mustard, mustard pickles.

4 pounds cooked shrimp
1 medium onion
Juice of 2 lemons
1½ cups olive oil
1½ cups white vinegar
Salt and pepper
1 tablespoon Worcestershire sauce
½ tablespoon Tabasco sauce
2 tablespoons prepared mustard
5 mustard pickles with 1 tablespoon of the sauce

Cut the shrimp into medium-sized pieces, and put aside. Slice the onion and marinate it in the juice of the lemons for about half an hour.

Sauce: Mix slowly the oil, vinegar, salt, and pepper and beat until thoroughly blended. Add the Worcestershire sauce and the Tabasco sauce. Pour off the lemon juice from the onions and mix it with the mustard and mustard pickle juice, and add to the oil and vinegar mixture. Mince the pickles, mix them with the onions, and add them to the sauce. Now add the shrimp and let the dish stand for several hours before serving so that the shrimp will absorb the pickle flavor.

Serves 8.

Overlooking the Danube, Budapest, Hungary

HUNGARY

BEEF STEW A LA MODE GUNDEL

YOU WILL NEED: beef, lard, flour, string beans, asparagus tips, sweet peas, goose liver, red wine, salt, pepper, marjoram, eggs, butter, sweet cream, French fried potatoes, parsley.

1¾ pounds tenderloin of beef, cut into strips
5½ ounces lard
1 ounce salt
Dash of pepper
Dash of marjoram
6½ ounces asparagus tips
6½ ounces sweet peas
6½ ounces French cut string beans
6½ ounces goose liver, cut into strips
4 ounces red wine
1 tablespoon flour

Scrambled-egg garnishing:
6 eggs
1¾ ounces butter
2 ounces sweet cream
Parsley
3 servings of French fried potatoes

Braise the tenderloin in the lard. Season with salt, pepper, and marjoram. Cook the asparagus tips, peas, and beans in salt water, and hold until ready to be used. As the meat becomes tender add the strips of goose liver. When cooked, add red wine, and thicken with a little sifted flour. Mix in the beans, peas, and the asparagus tips. Top stew with a nest-like arrangement of scrambled eggs made with butter and cream. Sprinkle with parsley. Serve with French fried potatoes.

Serves 4.

Tananger Bay, Norway

Norway

FERSK SUPPE OG KJTT
(Beef with Carrots and Cabbage)

YOU WILL NEED: beef marrow bones, beef, dried oxtail soup, salt, pepper, carrots, cabbage, parsley, stock, onion, wine vinegar, sugar, flour.

2 pounds beef marrow bones
2¼ quarts water
3 pounds chuck beef
1 packet dried oxtail soup
2½ teaspoons salt
⅓ teaspoon pepper
6 large carrots, sliced
1 small head cabbage, cut into strips
Sauce:
½ pint stock
1 small onion, chopped
4 teaspoons wine vinegar
2 teaspoons sugar
1 tablespoon flour

Boil the bones in the water in a large heavy pan for 1½ to 2 hours. Remove the bones. Add the meat and the dried oxtail soup to the stock and simmer until the meat is tender, or for about 2 hours. Strain and chill the stock so that the fat can be easily removed. Return the meat to the stock; add the salt, pepper, carrots, and cabbage; cook until the vegetables are tender. Remove the meat, carrots, and cabbage. Serve the meat sliced with carrots, cabbage, and sauce.

Sauce: Simmer the stock and the onion until the onion is tender. Add the vinegar, sugar, and flour, and stir until the sauce thickens.

Serves 6.

Rural Village, Korea

KOREA

BUKOKI (PUL-KOGGI) (Beef)

YOU WILL NEED: beef, sugar, oil, soy sauce, pepper, green onion, garlic, sesame seeds, flour.

1 pound beef
4 tablespoons sugar
5 tablespoons oil
6 tablespoons soy sauce
Pepper
1 green onion, chopped, including top
1 clove garlic, chopped
4 tablespoons prepared sesame seeds
1 tablespoon flour
Water

Cut the beef into thin slices 3 inches square. Combine the sugar and oil, and mix well. Combine the soy sauce, pepper, onion, garlic, prepared sesame seeds, and flour. Add this mixture to the meat, and mix well. Let stand for 15 minutes. Fry the meat in a small amount of the oil until well browned. Add a small amount of water, cover the pan tightly, and steam until the meat is tender. Serve hot.

Serves 2.

Kandy, Ceylon

Ceylon

YELLOW RICE

YOU WILL NEED: rice, fat, cloves, cardamom seeds, bay leaves, onion, turmeric, salt, chicken stock.

1 cup long grain rice
3 to 5 tablespoons fat (margarine, corn oil, or butter)
2 cloves
4 cardamom seeds
2 to 3 bay leaves
1 large onion, chopped
Pinch of turmeric
1 teaspoon salt
1½ to 2 cups water or chicken stock

Wash and drain the rice. Boil, drain, and wash to remove excess starch if any. Heat the fat; add all the ingredients except the turmeric, salt, and liquid; fry until the onion is golden. Add the rice, turmeric, and salt and fry for a minute or two. Add the water or stock. Cook until the rice is cooked through. Reduce the temperature and simmer or place in an oven until the rice is fluffy and grainy and the water is absorbed.

Remove the cloves, cardamom, and bay leaves; place the rice on a serving platter and garnish with any one of the following:
a) fried parsley or celery leaves
b) slices of fried bacon
c) chopped hard-boiled egg or shredded fried omelet
d) boiled peas

Serves 4.

The Acropolis & Parthenon, Athens, Greece

GREECE

MOUSSAKA

YOU WILL NEED: eggplants, butter, ground beef, onions, tomato paste, parsley, red wine, salt, pepper, cinnamon, eggs, Parmesan cheese, bread crumbs, milk, nutmeg, cooking oil.

4 medium eggplants
Salt
4 tablespoons butter
2 pounds ground beef
3 onions, chopped
2 tablespoons tomato paste
¼ cup parsley, chopped
½ cup red wine
Salt and pepper
½ cup water
Dash cinnamon
3 eggs, beaten
½ cup Parmesan cheese, grated
½ cup bread crumbs
6 tablespoons butter
6 tablespoons flour
3 cups hot milk
Salt and pepper to taste
Dash nutmeg
4 egg yolks, lightly beaten
½ to ¾ cup cooking oil

Remove ½-inch-wide strips of peel lengthwise from the eggplants, leaving ½-inch peel between the strips. Cut the eggplants into thick slices, sprinkle with salt, and let stand between 2 heavy plates while browning the meat and making the sauce.

In a frying pan melt the 4 tablespoons of butter and sauté the meat and onions until the meat is browned. Add the tomato paste, parsley, wine, salt and pepper, and water. Simmer until the liquid is absorbed. Cool. Stir in the cinnamon, eggs, cheese, and half the bread crumbs.

Sauce: In a saucepan melt the 6 tablespoons of butter over low heat. Add flour and stir until well blended. Remove from heat. Gradually stir in the milk. Return to heat and cook, stirring, until the sauce is thick and smooth. Add salt and pepper to taste and the nutmeg. Combine the egg yolks with a little of the hot sauce, then stir the egg mixture into the sauce and cook over very low heat for 2 minutes, stirring constantly.

Brown the eggplant slices on both sides in hot oil. Grease an ovenproof casserole and sprinkle the bottom with the remaining bread crumbs. Cover the crumbs with a layer of eggplant slices, then a layer of meat and continue until all the eggplant and meat is used, finishing with a layer of eggplant. Cover with sauce, sprinkle with additional Parmesan cheese and bake in a 350-degree oven for 1 hour. Serve hot.

Serves 10.

Bogota Falls, Colombia

COLOMBIA

SOBREBARRIGA (Flank Steak)

YOU WILL NEED: flank steak, tomatoes, onion, carrot, garlic, bay leaf, parsley, thyme, oregano, salt, pepper, butter, bread crumbs.

2 pounds flank steak
2 medium tomatoes, chopped
1 medium onion, chopped
1 carrot, chopped
2 cloves garlic, chopped
1 bay leaf
Sprigs of parsley
¾ teaspoon thyme
¾ teaspoon oregano
Salt and pepper to taste
Water
4 tablespoons butter
¾ cup bread crumbs

In a large saucepan combine the meat with the tomatoes, onion, carrot, garlic, bay leaf, parsley, thyme, oregano, salt, and pepper. Cover the meat with water, and cook over very low heat for about 2 hours, or until the meat is tender. Remove the beef and dry it with paper towels. Reserve the liquid. Put the meat in a broiling pan, fat side up, spread it with soft butter, and cover it with the bread crumbs. Broil until the bread crumbs are golden brown. Slice and serve. Strain the seasoned liquid, and serve it in a saucebowl.

Serves 4.

Sea of Galilee, Israel

ISRAEL

JAFFA DUCK (Roast Duck in Orange Sauce)

YOU WILL NEED: duck, oranges, sugar, corn flour.

2 ducks, cleaned
6 oranges
2 ounces sugar
2 ounces corn flour

Warm a greased baking dish in a medium oven, add the cleaned ducks, and roast them for 1 hour, turning occasionally. Extract the juice from 5 oranges. Dissolve the sugar in a saucepan, and cook, until dark brown. Add the orange juice. Dilute the corn flour with water, and add to the sugar and juice mixture while stirring. Continue to boil the sauce for 3 minutes, stirring constantly. Arrange cut pieces of duck on a platter. Pour on the orange sauce, and decorate the dish with circular orange slices. Serve with steamed cabbage, garden peas, and roast potatoes arranged on a separate serving dish.

Serves 8.

Bamboo Avenue, Jamaica

JAMAICA

BONED STUFFED FISH

YOU WILL NEED: fish, lime juice, salt, pepper, bread crumbs, onion, parsley, butter.

- **1 fish, about 3½ to 4 pounds** (snapper, Jack or King fish)
- **3 tablespoons lime juice**
- **1½ teaspoon salt**
- **1 teaspoon pepper**
- **3 cups bread crumbs**
- **2 tablespoons onion, chopped**
- **2 teaspoons parsley, chopped**
- **3 tablespoons butter, melted**

Prepare the fish for cooking. Remove the backbone with a very sharp knife. Rub two tablespoons of lime juice over the fish. Rub the inside and outside of the fish with salt and pepper. Combine the crumbs, onion, parsley, lime juice, and 1 tablespoon of butter. Fill the body cavity and the space from which the bone was taken with the mixture. Close up the cavity with a needle and thread. Smear the fish with a little fat. Bake it in a moderate oven until done. Sprinkle the fish with some buttered bread crumbs and return it to the oven for a few minutes. Garnish with lime slices and onion rings.

Serves 6.

Coastline, Yugoslavia

YUGOSLAVIA

SVINJSKI PAPRIKAS SA KISELIM KUPUSOM I PAVLAKOM (Pork Stew with Sauerkraut and Cream)

YOU WILL NEED: pork, onions, lard, sauerkraut, pepper, paprika, salt, sour cream.

2 pounds pork
5 ounces onions, finely chopped
⅔ cup lard
2 pounds sauerkraut, finely chopped
Pepper
Paprika
Salt
1 cup sour cream

Wash the meat and cut it into 1-inch cubes. Fry 3 ounces of the chopped onions in ⅓ cup of lard; add the sauerkraut. Fry until the sauerkraut is tender, adding water in small quantities. Put the remaining ⅓ cup of lard into large skillet, add 2 ounces of chopped onions and the meat, and fry for about 40 minutes, or until the meat is tender. Mix the sauerkraut and the meat; add pepper, paprika, a little water, and salt, and let the stew simmer for 29 minutes. When nearly done, pour ½ cup of sour cream over the dish. Pour on the remaining ½ cup of sour cream just before serving.

Serves 4

Moon-watching shrine, Kyoto, Japan

SUKIYAKI

YOU WILL NEED: beef suet, beef tenderloin, MSG, sugar, Japanese soy sauce, sake, beef bouillon, scallions or green onions, Chinese cabbage, mushrooms, spinach leaves, tofu (bean curd), bamboo shoots, shirataki (thin bean thread noodles).

4 ounces beef suet
3 pounds beef tenderloin, very thinly sliced
1 teaspoon MSG
⅓ cup sugar
½ cup Japanese soy sauce
¼ cup sake (dry vermouth or sherry may be substituted)
1 cup beef bouillon
12 scallions or green onions, cut into 2-inch lengths
½ head Chinese cabbage, thinly sliced (one celery heart with leaves can be substituted)
12 large mushrooms, thinly sliced
1 pound fresh spinach leaves, cut into 1-inch strips
12 1-inch cubes of tofu— (if cannot be obtained, simply omit)
1 can bamboo shoots, cut into bite-sized pieces
6 ounces shirataki
All the ingredients should be attractively arranged on platters in advance.

Preheat an electric frying pan or heat a heavy iron skillet on an electric hot plate at the dining table. Cut the suet into small pieces and melt it until there are about 2 tablespoons of fat; remove the suet.

Place the meat in the pan; as soon as one side turns color, turn and brown lightly on the other side. Sprinkle the meat with ½ teaspoon of MSG and ⅓ cup of sugar; add ½ cup of soy sauce, ¼ cup of sake and about half of the bouillon. Push the meat aside.

Into the bubbling sauce add the onions, Chinese cabbage, and mushrooms, keeping them divided into separate groups as much as possible. Continue cooking and gently turn each group so all of the ingredients become soaked in the sauce and are steamed through. Still keeping ingredients separated, push aside and add the spinach, tofu (if available), bamboo shoots, and shirataki.

It is a matter of individual taste when Sukiyaki is done. It is best to begin eating, with each person helping himself, as soon as the vegetables have been heated through. They should be slightly crisp and not allowed to "stew" in the hot sauce. While the first serving is being eaten, the remaining uncooked Sukiyaki may be put into the pan and the entire process repeated. Sukiyaki should be accompanied by plain steamed rice served in a separate dish.

Serves 4.

Halstatt, Austria

Austria

WIENER ROSTBRATEN (Viennese Steaks)

YOU WILL NEED: onions, butter, beef sirloin, vegetable oil, salt, black pepper, beef stock, parsley, bacon.

6 medium onions, peeled and thinly sliced
6 tablespoons butter
3 pounds boneless beef sirloin, cut ½ inch thick, then pounded to ¼ inch thick
3 tablespoons vegetable oil
Salt
Freshly ground black pepper
½ cup beef stock, fresh or canned
Parsley, chopped
6 slices bacon, fried

Cut the sliced onion into strips ⅛ to ¼ inch wide. In a heavy 8- or 10-inch skillet over medium heat, melt 4 tablespoons of the butter; add the onions. Stirring occasionally, cook them for 8 to 10 minutes, or until they are colored and crisp. Add more butter if necessary while the onions are frying—they must not burn. Set the onions aside, uncovered, in the skillet.

Cut the steak into 6 equal portions. In a 10- or 12-inch heavy skillet, heat the oil and the remaining 2 tablespoons of butter over medium heat. When the butter foam subsides, add the steaks. Raise the heat to moderately high and cook the steaks briskly for 2 to 4 minutes, depending upon the degree of doneness you prefer. Arrange the steaks on a heated platter and sprinkle them with salt and a few grindings of pepper.

Add the stock to the skillet in which the steaks were cooked, and bring it to a boil, stirring in any brown bits clinging to the pan, then pour the sauce over the steaks. Reheat the onions over high heat for a minute or so to restore their crispness. Serve the steaks with a mound of onions placed on each one. Then garnish with chopped parsley and crumbled bacon sprinkled over the onions.

Serves 6.

Tomb of Hafiz, Iran

MORG POLO (Chicken with Rice)

YOU WILL NEED: rice, salt, chicken, black pepper, cinnamon, poultry seasoning, butter, onions, raisins, dried apricots.

Rice:

4 cups raw long grain rice
3 tablespoons salt
3 quarts water

Chicken:

3 pounds chicken breasts
1½ teaspoons salt
½ teaspoon black pepper
½ teaspoon cinnamon
1 teaspoon poultry seasoning
½ pound butter
1¾ cups onions, chopped
1 cup raisins
1 cup dried apricots, chopped

Place the rice in a strainer and wash it under warm water for 5 minutes. Put the rice in a saucepan, cover it with cold water, and add half the salt. Let the rice soak for 2 hours, then drain. Bring the 3 quarts of water and the remaining salt to a boil. Add the rice and cook over medium heat for 12 minutes. Drain and rinse with lukewarm water. Prepare the chicken while the rice is soaking.

Wash and dry the chicken; rub it with salt, pepper, cinnamon, and poultry seasoning. Melt 3 tablespoons of butter in a skillet, and sauté the onions until brown; remove the onions. Melt 5 tablespoons of butter in the same skillet, brown the chicken pieces, and remove them. Soak the raisins and apricots in warm water for 5 minutes, drain well, and sauté in the fat for 5 minutes.

Melt the remaining butter. Put 3 tablespoons of it into a large casserole, add 3 tablespoons of water, and spread half the rice on the bottom. Arrange the chicken, onions, and fruits over the rice, and cover with the remaining rice. Pour the remaining butter over the top. Place a piece of foil over the top and edges of the casserole to seal. Bake in a 300-degree oven for 45 minutes.

Serves 6.

Index

21 CHILE
EMPANADAS DE HORNO
YOU WILL NEED: onions, ground beef, shortening, paprika, salt, pepper, flour, beef broth, eggs, black olives, raisins.

75 CHINA
SWEET AND SOUR PORK
YOU WILL NEED: pork, salt, pepper, sesame oil, sherry, cornstarch, peanut oil, egg, water, sugar, malt vinegar, tomato ketchup, pineapple cubes, red chili pepper, green peppers, pickled cabbage, carrot, cucumber.

107 COLOMBIA
SOBREBARRIGA (Flank Steak)
YOU WILL NEED: flank steak, tomatoes, onion, carrot, garlic, bay leaf, parsley, thyme, oregano, salt, pepper, butter, bread crumbs.

53 CZECHOSLOVAKIA
PORK CHOPS A LA BRATISLAVA
YOU WILL NEED: pork chops, salt, pepper, shortening, green peppers, onion, tomatoes, caraway seeds, butter.

27 DENMARK
FLAESKESTEG MED RDKAL (Roast Ham with Red Cabbage)
YOU WILL NEED: ham, coarse salt, ginger, Gravy Master, potatoes, sugar, butter, pickled cucumber, red cabbage, red currant juice.

95 ECUADOR
SEAFOOD IN PICKLE SAUCE
YOU WILL NEED: shrimp, onion, lemons, olive oil, white vinegar, salt, pepper, Worcestershire sauce, Tabasco sauce, prepared mustard, mustard pickles.

59 ENGLAND
YORKSHIRE BEEF HOTPOT
YOU WILL NEED: stewing beef, flour, salt, oil, onion, Bovril, potatoes, Lancashire cheese (optional).

91 FINLAND
KESAEKEITTO (Summer Vegetable Soup)
YOU WILL NEED: carrots, potatoes, peas, cauliflower, spinach, sugar, nutmeg, salt, flour, milk, prawns, parsley.

55 FRANCE
GIGOT D'AGNEAU AUX MARRONS (Leg of Lamb with Chestnuts)
YOU WILL NEED: lamb, salt, pepper, flour, chestnut puree, onions, chicken broth, white wine, bread crumbs, butter.

25 GERMANY
KALBSHAXE (Veal Shank)
YOU WILL NEED: carrots, onions, celery, salt, pepper, stock, veal, butter, bay leaf.

105 GREECE
MOUSSAKA
YOU WILL NEED: eggplants, butter, ground beef, onions, tomato paste, parsley, red wine, salt, pepper, cinnamon, eggs, Parmesan cheese, bread crumbs, milk, nutmeg, cooking oil.

HOLLAND

83 **RUNDERLAPPEN (Pickled Steaks)**

YOU WILL NEED: round steak, salt, pepper, butter or oil, onions, wine vinegar, mustard, bay leaf, cloves, peppercorns.

HUNGARY

97 **BEEF STEW A LA MODE GUNDEL**

YOU WILL NEED: beef, lard, flour, string beans, asparagus tips, sweet peas, goose liver, red wine, salt, pepper, marjoram, eggs, butter, sweet cream, French fried potatoes, parsley.

INDIA

85 **CHILLI CHICKEN**

YOU WILL NEED: chicken, salt, red pepper, black pepper, eggs, flour, white mushrooms, salad oil, cucumber, spring onion, garlic, ginger, chilli peppers, vinegar, stock, sherry, sugar, soya-bean sauce, Ve-Tsin, white pepper.

INDONESIA

43 **SATE (Lamb Shishkebab)**

YOU WILL NEED: lamb, vinegar, garlic, peanut butter, milk, bouillon broth, red pepper, soy sauce, sugar, bay leaf, salt.

IRAN

121 **MORG POLO (Chicken with Rice)**

YOU WILL NEED: rice, salt, chicken, black pepper, cinnamon, poultry seasoning, butter, onions, raisins, dried apricots.

IRELAND

23 **DUBLIN CODDLE (Stew of Bacon and Sausage)**

YOU WILL NEED: pork sausages, bacon, onions, potatoes, parsley, salt, pepper.

ISRAEL

109 **JAFFA DUCK (Roast Duck in Orange Sauce)**

YOU WILL NEED: duck, oranges, sugar, corn flour.

ITALY

51 **SPAGHETTI ALLA MOLISANA**

YOU WILL NEED: onion, butter, Prosciutto, parsley, basil, red pepper, garlic, oregano, salt, tomatoes, spaghetti, Romano cheese.

JAMAICA

111 **BONED STUFFED FISH**

YOU WILL NEED: fish, lime juice, salt, pepper, bread crumbs, onion, parsley, butter.

JAPAN

117 **SUKIYAKI**

YOU WILL NEED: beef suet, beef tenderloin, MSG, sugar, Japanese soy sauce, sake, beef bouillon, scallions or green onions, Chinese cabbage, mushrooms, spinach leaves, tofu (bean curd), bamboo shoots, shirataki (thin bean thread noodles).

JORDAN

47 **WARAK INIB MIHSHEE (Grape Leaf Rolls)**

YOU WILL NEED: grape leaves, lemons, lamb bones, rice, lamb, salt, pepper.

101 KOREA

BUKOKI (PUL-KOGGI) (Broiled Beef)

YOU WILL NEED: beef, sugar, oil, soy sauce, pepper, green onion, garlic, sesame seeds, flour.

89 MEXICO

CHICKEN MOLE

YOU WILL NEED: butter, chicken, salt, chicken broth, green pepper, sesame seeds, garlic, cloves, cinnamon, pepper, coriander, unsweetened chocolate, almonds, chili powder, tomatoes, rice, pimentos.

49 MOROCCO

DJAJ M'KALLI
(Chicken with Lemon and Olives)

YOU WILL NEED: chicken, garlic, salt, vegetable oil, ginger, turmeric, black pepper, saffron, salt, onions, butter, garlic, Greek Kalamata olives, pickled lemons*.

99 NORWAY

FERSK SUPPE OG KJTT
(Beef with Carrots and Cabbage)

YOU WILL NEED: beef marrow bones, beef, dried oytail soup, salt, pepper, carrots, cabbage, parsley, stock, onion, wine vinegar, sugar, flour.

57 PERU

ARROZ CON PATO (Rice with Duck)

YOU WILL NEED: duck, pork, lard, onion, tomatoes, garlic, salt, parsley, chili powder, rice, peas, brandy.

81 PHILIPPINE ISLANDS

CHICKEN AND PORK ADOBO
(Braised Chicken and Pork)

YOU WILL NEED: chicken, pork, vinegar, garlic, soy sauce, salt, pepper, lard.

19 POLAND

ZRAZY A LA NELSON II

YOU WILL NEED: butter, onion, bouillon, mushrooms, potatoes, veal, salt, pepper, sour cream, red wine.

35 PORTUGAL

BACALHAU (Codfish, Portuguese Style)

YOU WILL NEED: eggs, potatoes, salt, cod, olive oil, garlic, onions, olives, seasoned salt, pepper, white wine, parsley.

17 PUERTO RICO

LANGOSTA A LA CRIOLLA-ESTILO PUERTORRIQUEÑO (Lobster Creole)

YOU WILL NEED: onions, green peppers, garlic, olive oil, salt, pepper, tomatoes, tomato sauce, lobster, white cooking wine.

41 RUSSIA

BEEF STROGANOFF

YOU WILL NEED: butter, flour, beef stock or condensed consommé, mustard, tomato paste, onion, mushrooms, beef, salt, pepper, sour cream, potatoes.

29 SAUDI ARABIA

KABSAH (Rice with Meat)

YOU WILL NEED: onions, butter, lamb, tomatoes, carrots, garlic, salt, black pepper, cardamom, rice.

93 SOUTH AFRICA
BOBOTIE
YOU WILL NEED: onions, apple, butter, lamb, beef, bread, curry powder, sugar, eggs, vinegar, salt, pepper, raisins, almonds, bay leaves, milk, turmeric (optional).

45 SPAIN
PAELLA A LA VALENCIANA
YOU WILL NEED: veal, pork, chicken, olive oil, garlic, onion, tomatoes, rice, clams, red peppers, crab meat, peas, lobster, artichoke hearts, saffron, garlic, salt, pepper.

39 SURINAM
KIPPENPASTEI (Chicken Pie)
YOU WILL NEED: flour, butter, chicken, onions, butter, bouillon cubes, salt, pepper, peas, carrots, capers, eggs.

87 SWEDEN
PLOMMONSPACKAD FLASKKARRE
(Loin of Pork with Prunes)
YOU WILL NEED: prunes, pork, salt, pepper, ginger.

67 SWITZERLAND
FONDUE SUPREME
YOU WILL NEED: Swiss cheese, Gruyère cheese, garlic, white wine, lemon juice, nutmeg, cornstarch, Kirsch, Italian or French bread, champagne, apples, pears, melon, grapes.

79 THAILAND
BEEF MUSSULMAN CURRY
YOU WILL NEED: beef, coconut cream*, peanuts, nam pia, curry paste, cinnamon, cardamom, tamarind pods, lime, palm sugar.

71 TRINIDAD
FRUITS DE MER A LA TRINIDAD
YOU WILL NEED: shrimp, lobster, snapper, oysters, mushrooms, onion, salt, Tabasco sauce, sherry wine, butter, flour, milk, Parmesan cheese, potatoes.

77 TURKEY
TURLU (Vegetable Pot)
YOU WILL NEED: onions, butter, lamb, tomatoes, zucchini, eggplant, okra, green peppers, salt and pepper, green beans.

61 VENEZUELA
HALLACAS (Corn Pie)
YOU WILL NEED: white cornmeal, butter, eggs, salt, chicken, pork, tomatoes, onion, parsley, garlic, capers, olives, raisins, cayenne pepper, black pepper, oregano, allspice, chilies.

115 YUGOSLAVIA
SVINJSKI PAPRIKAS SA KISELIM KUPUSOM I PAVLAKOM (Pork Stew with Sauerkraut and Cream)
YOU WILL NEED: pork, onions, lard, sauerkraut, pepper, paprika, salt, sour cream.

ACKNOWLEDGEMENTS

The author wishes to extend grateful thanks and appreciation to the following for their assistance in the preparation of this book.

Swiss Center Restaurant Inc.

Yugoslavia State Tourist Office

Austrian Airlines

Irish Tourist Board

Embassy of the Hungarian Peoples Republic

Greek National Tourist Organization

Italian Government Travel Office

The Netherlands Information Service

French Government Tourist Office

British Information Service

Official Belgium Tourist Office

Bulgarian Tourist Office

Hotel Plaza Grill, Madrid, Spain

Consulate General of Denmark

Lufthansa German Airlines

Polish Embassy

Czechoslovak Travel Bureau

Canadian Government Travel Bureau

Embassy of Sweden

Surinam Tourist Bureau

Embassy of Colombia

Jamaican Embassy

Embassy of Indonesia

China Airlines, Ltd.

Japan Airlines

The Royal Afghan Embassy

Air-India

The Embassy of the Union of Burma

Embassy of Ceylon

Tourist Organization of Thailand

Philippine Embassy

Embassy of Australia

Plaza Hotel Grill, Buenos Aires, Argentina

South African Embassy

Restaurant Lima Las Trece Monedas, Lima, Peru

Embassy of Chile

Embassy of Venezuela

Ecuadorian Embassy

Embassy of Korea

Turkish Embassy

Embassy of Jordan

Embassy of Morocco

Israel Information Service

Saudi Arabia Embassy

PHOTO CREDITS

PAGE	COUNTRY	PHOTOGRAPHER
16	Puerto Rico	Margaret Troy
18	Poland	Andy Bernhaut
20	Chile	Susan McCartney
22	Ireland	Fritz Henle
24	Germany	Susan McCartney
26	Denmark	Fritz Henle
28	Saudi Arabia	Tom Hollyman
30	Afghanistan	Stephanie Dinkins
32	Burma	Van Bucher
34	Portugal	George Holton
36	Bulgaria	Teresa Zabala
38	Surinam	Fritz Henle
40	Russia	John Lewis Stage
42	Indonesia	John Lewis Stage
44	Spain	John Lewis Stage
46	Jordan	Sid Latham
48	Morocco	George Holton
50	Italy	John Ross
52	Czechoslovakia	George Holton
54	France	John Ross
56	Peru	George Holton
58	England	John Lewis Stage
60	Venezuela	John Lewis Stage
62	Canada	John Lewis Stage
64	Argentina	Carl Frank
66	Switzerland	H. Steiner
68	Brazil	Carl Frank
70	Trinidad	Fritz Henle
72	Belgium	P. Berger
74	China	George Holton
76	Turkey	Fritz Henle
78	Thailand	Van Bucher
80	Philippines	John Lewis Stage
82	Holland	Margaret Troy
84	India	George Holton
86	Sweden	John Lewis Stage
88	Mexico	John Lewis Stage
90	Finland	Fritz Henle
92	South Africa	Arthur Griffin
94	Ecuador	Stephanie Dinkins
96	Hungary	Glauboch
98	Norway	John Lewis Stage
100	Korea	Carl Purcell
102	Ceylon	George Holton
104	Greece	George Berben
106	Colombia	Mort Beebe
108	Israel	Jerry Cooke
110	Jamaica	Aurthur Griffin
112	Australia	John Lewis Stage
114	Yugoslavia	John Lewis Stage
116	Japan	John Lewis Stage
118	Austria	Tony La Tona
120	Iran	Fred Maroon